SELF-EDITING FOR FICTION WRITERS

SELF-EDITING

....

FOR FICTION

....

WRITERS

....

RENNI BROWNE AND

DAVE KING

ILLUSTRATIONS BY GEORGE BOOTH

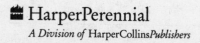
HarperPerennial

A Division of HarperCollins*Publishers*

A hardcover edition of this book was published in 1993 by HarperCollins Publishers.

Illustrations for Chapters 1 through 11 copyright © 1993 by George Booth.
Illustration for Chapter 12: Drawing by Booth; copyright © 1991 The New Yorker Magazine, Inc.

HarperCollins books may be purchased for educational, business, or sales promotional use. For information please write: Special Markets Department, Harper-Collins Publishers, Inc., 10 East 53rd Street, New York, NY 10022.

FIRST HARPERPERENNIAL EDITION published 1994

Designed by Jessica Shatan

The Library of Congress has catalogued the hardcover edition as follows:

Browne, Renni.
  Self-editing for fiction writers / Renni Browne and Dave King. — 1st ed.
    p.   cm.
    Includes bibliographical references.
    ISBN 0-06-270061-8
    1. Fiction—Technique. 2. Editing. I. King, Dave, 1960—   . II.Title.
  PN 162.B74   1993
  808.3—dc20   92-11229

ISBN 0-06-272046-5

    96   97   98   RRD   10   9

CONTENTS

ACKNOWLEDGMENTS
....

Even editors, when they are writing, need editors. We get as close to our work—and need as much support—as the authors we work with. As soon as we had something that looked like a draft, we passed it around to the other members of The Editorial Department. We would like to thank all of them for their editing, encouragement, hand-holding, and harassment. And to single out:

Jane Rafal, who more than anyone else kept the fires lit under us.

Judith Searle, who supplied inspiration and examples from the West Coast office.

John Maloney, mystery editor and Scrabble™ player extraordinaire, whose careful copyreading of the final draft kept us from infelicities of expression that might have come back to haunt us.

Alison Whyte, who kept the promotional material we were asked to write about ourselves from being implausibly modest.

And last, but not least, the company cats (Tyrone, Pandora, the Mop, Jessie, Spike, Maggie the Cat, Molly, Mimi, Fluffy, and the late, lamented Dudley) all of whom graciously agreed not to walk over any word processor that had material intended for this book on its screen.

Also, Boothie the wonder dog, whose irresistibility persuaded her namesake to illustrate this book for us.

INTRODUCTION

Why self-editing?

Because self-editing is probably the only kind of editing your manuscript will ever get.

Not too many years ago, an author with obvious talent and style sold a novel or short-story collection to a publishing house and then revised it under the guidance of the editor who signed the book up. Gifted editors routinely spent enormous amounts of creative energy and blue-pencil lead to bring the manuscript to its fullest potential.

That was then. What about today? What actually happens to the fiction manuscripts that come in to publishing houses?

If the plot is strong enough or topical enough or the characters engaging enough, the manuscript is signed up and put into print—"potential" be damned.

If the fiction technique seems amateurish, or the plot doesn't hold the reader from page one to the end, or the characters don't stay in the mind after you close the book, the manuscript is rejected—potential be damned.

Which is why well-established fiction writers who used to get thoughtful, supportive editing now feel ignored when their manuscripts are put into production as submitted. And why first-time authors are being printed rather than published—assuming they're fortunate enough to get a publishing contract in the first place.

"These days, many writers lack faith in the editing process at publishing houses," Edwin McDowell wrote in a New York Times article on independent book editors. "Other writers, novices, want their manuscripts polished before they even submit them. And the recent cutbacks and consolidations at publishing houses have left many of those houses editorially shorthanded."

Author loyalty isn't what it used to be. It no longer pays a publishing house to develop a manuscript to its fullest potential and its author to fame and/or fortune. Authors who sell well are almost certain to go to the highest bidder, and publishers can't reasonably afford to develop an author for a competing house.

Nor are editors what they used to be. An acquisitions editor who signs up fifteen or twenty books a year couldn't possibly edit all of them, even if encouraged to do so. And one of the casualties of recent publishing evolution is the apprenticeship system by which editing used to be taught. The only way, really, to learn editing is to learn it from another editor.

Which is what you'll be doing with this book. We aren't going to tell you how to plot your novel or develop your characters. What we're going to do is teach you the craft of editing. The mechanics of dialogue, point of view, interior monologue; the tricks to striking the most effective balance between narrative summary and immediate scenes; the techniques whose adoption brands your manuscript as the work of a professional instead of an amateur.

Our purpose is to train you to see your manuscript the way an editor might see it—to do for yourself what a publishing-house editor once might have done. Exercises and examples will show you how to become an editor as well as a writer.

A word of warning: writing and editing are two different processes requiring two different mind sets. Don't try to do both at once. The time to edit is not while you're writing your first draft. But once that first draft is finished, you can use the principles in this book to increase—dramatically—the effectiveness of the story you've told and the way you've told it.

What's being covered is the aspect of writing that creative writing programs and books—concerned with the art of writing—most often overlook: editing. Because the way to learn editing is, still, to learn it from another editor.

CHAPTER 1

....

SHOW AND TELL

What's wrong with this paragraph:

> The conversation was barely begun before I discovered that our host was more than simply a stranger to most of his guests. He was an enigma, a mystery. And this was a crowd that doted on mysteries. In the space of no more than five minutes, I heard several different people put forth their theories—all equally probable or preposterous—as to who and what he was. Each theory was argued with the kind of assurance that can only come from a lack of evidence, and it seemed that, for many of the guests, these arguments were the main reason to attend his parties.

In a sense, of course, there is nothing wrong. The paragraph is grammatically impeccable. It describes the mystery surrounding the party's host clearly, efficiently, and with a sense of style. The writing is smooth.

Now look at the same passage as it actually appeared in F.

Scott Fitzgerald's *The Great Gatsby*:

> "I like to come," Lucille said. "I never care what I do, so I always have a good time. When I was here last, I tore my gown on a chair, and he asked me my name and address—within a week I got a package from Croirier's with a new evening gown in it."
>
> "Did you keep it?" asked Jordan.
>
> "Sure I did. I was going to wear it tonight, but it was too big in the bust and had to be altered. It was gas blue with lavender beads. Two hundred and sixty-five dollars."
>
> "There's something funny about a fellow that'll do a thing like that," said the other girl eagerly. "He doesn't want any trouble with *any*body."
>
> "Who doesn't?" I inquired.
>
> "Gatsby. Somebody told me—"
>
> The two girls and Jordan leaned together confidentially.
>
> "Somebody told me they thought he killed a man."
>
> A thrill passed over all of us. The three Mr. Mumbles bent forward and listened eagerly.
>
> "I don't think it's so much *that*," argued Lucille skeptically; "it's more that he was a German spy during the war."
>
> One of the men nodded in confirmation.
>
> "I heard that from a man who knew all about him, grew up with him in Germany," he assured us positively.
>
> "Oh, no," said the first girl, "it couldn't be that, because he was in the American army during the war." As our credulity switched back to her, she leaned forward with enthusiasm. "You look at him sometimes when he thinks nobody's looking at him. I'll bet he killed a man."

What's the difference between these two examples? To put it simply, it's a matter of showing and telling. The first paragraph is narrative summary, with no specific setting or characters. We are simply *told* about the guests' love of mystery, the weakness of the arguments, the conviction of the arguers. In the second version we actually get to see the breathless partygoers putting forth their theories and can almost taste the eagerness of their audience. The first version is a second-hand report. The second is an immediate scene.

What, exactly, constitutes a scene? For one thing it takes place in real time. Your readers are seeing events as they unfold, whether those events are a group discussion of the merits of Woody Allen films, a lone man running from an assassin, or a woman lying in a field pondering the meaning of life. In scenes, events are seen as they happen rather than described after the fact.

Scenes usually have settings as well, specific locations that the readers can picture. In Victorian novels these settings were often described in exhaustive (and exhausting) detail. Nowadays literature is leaner and meaner, and it's a good idea to give your readers only enough detail to help them picture your settings for themselves.

Scenes also contain some action, something that happens. Mary kills Harry, or Harry and Mary beat each other up. More often than not, what happens is dialogue between one or more characters. Though even in dialogue scenes it's a good idea to include a little physical action from time to time—what we call "beats"—to remind your readers of where your characters are and what they're doing. We'll be talking about beats at length in chapter seven.

Of course, anything that can go into a scene can also be summarized. And since scenes are usually harder to write than summaries, most authors rely too heavily on narrative summary to tell their stories. The result is often page after page, sometimes chapter after chapter, of writing that reads the way the first passage quoted above reads: clearly, perhaps even stylishly, but with no specific setting, no specific characters, no dialogue.

A century or so ago this sort of writing would have been fine. It was the norm, in fact—Henry James wrote at least one entire novel largely composed of narrative summary. But thanks to the influence of movies and television, readers today have become accustomed to seeing a story as a series of immediate scenes. Narrative summary no longer engages readers the way it once did.

Since engagement is exactly what a fiction writer wants to

accomplish, you're well advised to rely primarily on immediate scenes to put your story across. You want to draw your readers into the world you've created, make them feel a part of it, make them forget where they are. And you can't do this effectively if you tell your readers about your world second-hand. You have to actually take them there.

Not long ago we worked on a novel featuring a law firm in which one of the new associates led a rebellion against the senior partners. The author introduced the new associate and two of his colleagues in the first chapter by describing their job interviews with the senior partners. The interviews were given as narrative summary—she simply told her readers what the law firm was looking for in a new associate, described the associates' education and histories, and explained why the firm hired them. She did include snippets of dialogue from the interviews, but since readers never found out who the other speaker was or where the conversations took place, there was nothing they could picture.

Since the first chapter is not the best place for narrative summary—you want to engage your readers in your plot early on—we suggested that the author turn these interviews into genuine scenes, set in the senior partner's offices, with extended conversations between the partners and the new associates. As a result, her readers got a much better feel for who the new associates were and a glimpse of the senior partners' humor and good nature. The book was off to a much more engaging start.

Showing your story to your readers through scenes will give your writing immediacy. It will also give your writing transparency. One of the easiest ways to look like an amateur is to use mechanics that call attention to themselves and away from the story. You want your readers to be so wrapped up in your story that they are not even aware the author exists. But when you switch to narrative summary—especially if you go on at length—it can sometimes seem as if you were breaking into the story to give your readers a lecture. And there is no quicker way to turn readers off than to lecture them. This is

"Maynard constantly strived for a sense of style and immediacy."

especially true if you are using narrative summary for exposition. To write exposition at length—your characters' pasts, or events that happened before the story began, or any information your readers might need to understand your plot—is to risk lecturing your readers. It is usually more effective to bring out all sorts of exposition through scenes.

This won't always be possible, of course, especially if you're writing historical or science fiction, both of which usually require a lot of exposition. But even so, you'd be surprised at how much exposition can be converted into scenes. Rather than describing the history of Hartsdale House, you can write a scene in which the present Lord Hartsdale points out some of the family portraits to his guests. Or rather than quoting an *Encyclopedia Galactica* article on how Llanu society is organized, you can simply drop your readers into the middle of that society and let them fend for themselves.

We recently edited a book about Antonio Vivaldi that was set, naturally, in eighteenth-century Venice. In order to follow the story the readers had to know some of the details of Venetian society in the late baroque era. But because the story was presented as the reminiscences of one of Vivaldi's students, it was difficult to work the information into the text. After all, why would the student write in detail about the society she lived in? As far as she was concerned, everybody knew what the *bocca di lione* was and how you gained admission to the Golden Book.

To solve this problem, the author created a frame story about a modern-day researcher who supposedly found the student's writings in an archive. The researcher would interrupt the student's story every once in a while to explain some of the background. But since the researcher's explanations were simply addressed to the readers, they read like the lectures they really were. We suggested that the author give the researcher a personality and turn his lectures into scenes.

The author liked the idea. In the next draft, she had cast herself in the role of the researcher, and the lectures became first-person accounts of how she was visited by the ghost of Vivaldi on a trip to Venice. Since her Vivaldi had a powerful character's voice ("That fool Mozart could roll around on the floor with the soprano between acts, and no one cares. I leave the pulpit once and it follows me forever."), her tour through Venetian society took on a new life. It was shown rather than told.

Even though immediate scenes are almost always more engaging than narrative summary, be careful when self-editing not to convert *all* your narrative summary into scenes. Narrative summary serves several good purposes in fiction, the main one being to vary the rhythm of your writing. Scenes are immediate and engaging, but scene after scene without a break can become relentless and exhausting, especially if you tend to write brief, intense scenes. Every once in a while you will want to slow things down, to give your readers a chance to catch their breath, and narration can be a good way to do this.

One of our authors was given to short scenes in which characters met, talked, and then parted. All of the dialogue was well written and advanced his story, but since the author reported only five minutes' worth of dialogue for each scene, it was as if he'd written his entire novel in five-minute chunks. Reading it was like jogging on railroad ties. He could have run some of his scenes together into longer scenes, of course (and, in fact, we suggested he do so), but the real solution was to use narrative summary to work some extra time into his scenes.

In the next draft he showed two characters meeting for dinner, summarized the dinner itself in a paragraph or two of narration, and then showed the five minutes of after-dinner conversation that were really crucial to the story. By simply adding a few paragraphs of narration, he could stretch the duration of some of his scenes out to two or three hours without two or three hours' worth of dialogue and action. As a result his book had a more expansive feel to it, and his readers had a chance to rest between snippets of dialogue.

Narrative summary can also be useful when you have a lot of repetitive action. Say you are writing a book about a track star in which your hero participates in several races. If you show all of these races as immediate scenes, eventually they all start to look alike. But if you summarize the first few races—have them happen offstage, in effect—then the one you eventually show as a scene will have real impact.

And then, some plot developments are simply not important enough to justify scenes. If an event involves only minor characters you might do better to summarize it rather than develop the characters to the point that you could write a convincing scene about them. Or if you have a minor event that leads up to a key scene, you might want to narrate the first event so that the scene, when it comes, will seem even more immediate by contrast.

We once worked on a short story in which the police were tracking a rather enigmatic suspect. In the course of the story, three events happened in quick succession: the police realized just what the suspect was up to, they captured him, and he escaped during interrogation in a surprising way. Since the emphasis of the story was on what the suspect was up to rather than on his actual capture, we suggested that the capture be written as narrative summary. By not developing the capture into a full-blown scene, the author was able to go almost directly from the first revelation to a second, more important revelation that comes during interrogation. The story moved at a faster pace, and the two important scenes were thrown into sharp relief because a key scene was given as narrative summary.

Up until this point, we've been talking about showing and telling on the large scale, about narrating what should be shown through immediate scenes. But even within scenes there are ways in which you may tell what you should show. The *Gatsby* scene quoted above (Fitzgerald's version) shows us how people reacted to Gatsby, and shows us effectively. But the author also *tells* us that the three Mr. Mumbles leaned forward "eagerly," that one girl spoke with enthusiasm, that a man nodded "in affirmation." Granted, stylistic conventions have changed since 1925, but still the telling detracts because it's not needed: we've already been shown what the author then proceeds to tell us.

Authors usually indulge in this sort of small-scale telling to put across character traits or emotions. After all, the primary aim of fiction is to get your readers so involved in the lives of your characters that they feel what your characters feel—and they can't do that unless you make your characters' feelings clear. So you tell them. "Bishop Pettibone was never a man to allow his religion to interfere with his private life." "Wilbur felt absolutely defeated." "Geraldine was horrified at the news."

But telling your readers about your characters' emotions is

not the best way to get your readers involved. Far better to show why your characters feel the way they do. Instead of saying "Amanda took one look at the hotel room and recoiled in disgust," describe the room in such a way that the readers feel the disgust for themselves.

It's more work this way, of course. It's easier to simply say "Erma was depressed" than to come up with some original bit of action that shows she's depressed. But if you have her take one bite of her favorite cake and push the rest away (or have her polish off the whole cake), you will have given your readers a far better feel for her depression than you could by simply describing it. It is nearly always best to resist the urge to explain (or, as we so often write it in manuscript margins, R.U.E.).

This tendency to describe a character's emotion may reflect a lack of confidence on the part of the author. And more often than not, authors tell their readers things already shown by dialogue and action—it's as if they're repeating themselves to make sure their readers get the point. So when you come across an explanation of a character's emotion, simply cut the explanation. If the emotion is still shown, then the explanation wasn't needed. If the emotion isn't shown, then rewrite the passage so that it is.

To show you what we mean, take one last look at the Fitzgerald scene, this time with the explanations taken out. (We've also made a few other editorial changes along principles you'll be learning later in the book.) You can see from the results just how good a job Fitzgerald has done in showing all the emotions he tagged for us unnecessarily:

"I like to come," Lucille said. "I never care what I do, so I always have a good time. When I was here last, I tore my gown on a chair, and he asked me my name and address—within a week I got a package from Croirier's with a new evening gown in it."

"Did you keep it?" asked Jordan.

"Sure I did. I was going to wear it tonight, but it was too big in the bust and had to be altered. It was gas blue with lavender beads. Two hundred and sixty-five dollars."

"There's something funny about a fellow that'll do a thing like that," said the other girl. "He doesn't want any trouble with *any-body*."

"Who doesn't?" I inquired.

"Gatsby. Somebody told me..."

The two girls and Jordan leaned their heads together.

"Somebody told me they thought he killed a man."

A thrill passed over all of us. The three Mr. Mumbles bent forward in their seats.

"I don't think it's so much *that*," Lucille said. "It's more that he was a German spy during the war."

One of the men nodded.

"I heard that from a man who knew all about him, grew up with him in Germany," he said.

"Oh, no," said the first girl, "it couldn't be that, because he was in the American army during the war. You look at him sometimes when he thinks nobody's looking at him. I'll bet he killed a man."

Even within descriptions that have nothing to do with character emotion, there are ways you can show rather than tell. Rather than telling your readers that your hero's car is an old broken-down wreck, you can show him twisting two bare wires together to turn on the headlights, or driving through a puddle and being sprayed from the holes in the floor. That way your readers can draw their conclusions about the car's condition for themselves.

And just to show that editors aren't the only ones who notice showing and telling imbalances, here's a quote from Frederick Busch's *Los Angeles Times* review of Peter Ackroyd's *Dickens: Life and Times:*

> The need to announce, along with a need to reinforce with comment what has just been clearly shown, results in tones more appropriate to Dickens' funnier re-creations of his father's pomposities: "So far had the young author already come"; "So did the real world enter Dickens' fiction"; "So did his life, interior and exterior, continue." Where was Ackroyd's editor?

Bear in mind that "show, don't tell" is not a hard and fast rule—in fact, none of the self-editing principles in this book should be treated as rules. There are going to be times when telling will create more engagement than showing. In the Fitzgerald example, for instance, the line "A thrill passed over all of us" is clearly telling. And yet this line, coming so close on the rumor that Gatsby may have killed a man, gives a flavor of cheap gossip to the scene that heightens its effect.

But in good fiction this sort of telling is the exception, and a rare exception at that. Because when you show your story rather than tell it, you treat your readers with respect. And that respect makes it easier for you to draw them into the world you've created.

CHECKLIST

•First, how often do you use narrative summary? Are there long passages where nothing happens in real time? Do the main events in your plot take place in summary or in scenes?

•If you do have too much narrative summary, which sections do you want to convert into scenes? Does any of it involve major characters, where a scene could be used to flesh out their personalities? Does any of your narrative summary involve major plot twists or surprises? If so, start writing some scenes.

•Do you have *any* narrative summary, or are you bouncing from scene to scene without pausing for breath?

•Are you describing your characters' feelings? Have you *told* us they're angry? irritated? morose? discouraged? puzzled? excited? happy? elated? suicidal? Keep an eye out for any places where you mention an emotion outside of dialogue. Chances are you're telling what you should show. Remember to R.U.E.

EXERCISES

Spot the telling in the following and convert it to showing. The answers (at least, our answers) appear at the back of the book:

A. "Mortimer? Mortimer?" Simon Hedges said. "Where are you?"

"Look up, you ninny. I'm on the roof."

"What in blue blazes are you doing perched up there?"

Mortimer Twill explained to Simon how his long-awaited cupola and weather vane had finally arrived. He just couldn't wait for Simon to install the gadgets, so Mortimer had decided to climb up to the roof and complete the installation himself. He was still sorting through the directions.

"Come on down before you kill yourself," Simon said. "I swear I'll put them up for you this afternoon."

B. I'd known Uncle Zeb for years, of course, but I didn't feel like I really knew him until that first time I walked into his shop. All that time I'd thought he was just kind of handy, but looking at his tools—hundreds of them—and what they were and the way they were organized, well, I could see he was a craftsman.

C. *If you're in an ambitious mood, take the following bit of narrative summary and convert it into a scene. Hint: feel free to create any characters or elaborate on the settings any way you would like.*
Once you got off Route 9W, though, you were in another world, a world where two streets never met at a

right angle, where streets, in fact, didn't exist. Instead, you had "courts," "terraces," "ways," a "landing" or two. And lining these street-like things were row on row of little houses that could be distinguished, it seemed, only by the lawn ornaments. Travelers who disappeared into the developments had been known to call taxis just to lead them out again.

CHAPTER 2

CHARACTERIZATION AND EXPOSITION

Eloise had always assumed she would grow up to live like her mother—a quiet, sensible life full of furniture wax, good nutritious breakfasts, and compulsive bed making. But her first college roommate, Randi, introduced her to a whole new world, a world where you didn't have to tidy up before you invited friends in, where you didn't have to squeeze the toothpaste carefully from the bottom, and where you didn't have to pick up an iron again for the rest of your natural life. Eloise felt like she had been granted a reprieve after eighteen years in the June Cleaver Institute for Neurotic Young Girls.

Now, after spending ten minutes rooting through a pile of clothes to find a blouse that wasn't too dirty, then crunching across the living room carpet to spend another five hunting up a clean cereal bowl, she began to think that maybe there was something to be said for her mother's lifestyle after all.

After reading these paragraphs, you know something—possibly something important—about Eloise, her personality and background. But do you care? Most readers will probably be unable to work up more than the mildest interest in this character the author is working so hard to put over.

You're likely to have spotted the culprit—there's a lot of narrative summary in that first paragraph—and may already have thought of a way to convert this material into a scene (you could have Eloise's mother make a surprise visit, for instance). And, yes, one of the problems with this passage is that it tells us what it could be showing. In fact, the show-and-tell principle underlies most of the self-editing points we talk about from now on. But there's a second problem here: the author introduces Eloise to his readers all at once and in depth—stopping the story, in effect, for a summary of her character.

A lot of writers seem to feel they have to give their readers a clear understanding of a new character before they can get on with their story. They never bring a character on stage without a short personality summary. Or else they introduce their characters with flashbacks to the childhood scenes that made them who they are—in effect, psychoanalyzing the characters for their readers.

It's often a good idea to include enough physical description to help your readers picture a new character, a few specific details that capture the look of a character ("A good-looking man in his fifties," for instance, is too vague to be interesting). But when it comes to your characters' personalities, it's much more effective to have these emerge from character action, reaction, and dialogue than from description. Your readers will find your story more engaging if they can meet your characters the way they meet people in real life: a little at a time, with all the attendant pleasure of gradual discovery.

In the passage at the beginning of this chapter, watching Eloise fish for clean clothes and crunch across her carpet is enough to tell us she's a slob. We don't need to know at this point how she became one. Later in the story, we could learn about her upbringing when her mother comes to visit. In other words we could get to know Eloise gradually, the way we would get to know her in real life.

Another reason to avoid thumbnail character sketches is that the personality traits you tell us about when you introduce a character will (we would hope) eventually be shown by the way the character acts in the story. After all, if you describe a character as an elegant society matron and then show her flicking food at her husband in a restaurant or picking her nose in church, your readers won't believe your description. If your characters actually act the way your summaries say they will, then the summaries aren't needed. If they don't, then the summaries are misleading. Either way, your fiction is likely to be much more effective without the character summaries.

Also, when you summarize your characters, you risk over-defining them to the point that they're boxed in by the characterization with no room to grow. Someone once asked Leonard Nimoy how he came to develop the complex relationship between Captain Kirk and Mr. Spock that was one of the chief strengths of the old *Star Trek* series. How had he gone about working out such a deep and authentic friendship beforehand? Nimoy simply said that he didn't—and in fact couldn't—work it out in advance. Had he consciously mapped out Spock's relationship to Kirk, that relationship would never have been any deeper than the plan he had worked out. Instead he played the character intuitively, and there was no limit to the depths the relationship could attain.

When you define your characters the minute you introduce them, you may be setting boundary lines that your readers will use to interpret your characters' actions for the rest of the book. But if you allow your readers to get to know your characters gradually, then each reader will interpret them in his or her own way, thus getting a deeper sense of who your characters are than you could ever give in a summary. Allowing your readers this sort of leeway in understanding your characters

"The dwarf! The dwarf! The damn dwarf hiding in the foot locker! A hundred pages, or so ago! What was his name?..."

enables you to reach a wider audience—and reach it far more effectively—than defining your characters before we get to know them, or analyzing them after we get to know them.

Finally, sketching out your characters for your readers is just plain obtrusive. It's a form of telling that is almost certain to make your readers aware that you the author are hard at work.

Some authors take a more subtle approach than simply describing a new character's personality—they describe each new character's history. They may even trace their characters' pasts in the course of the story to two or three generations. It's perfectly understandable that an author should undertake this sort of historical characterization—delving into a character's past can be a good way for you to understand the character in the present. But though it may have been helpful for you to write a character's history, it may not be necessary for your readers to read it. Once you understand a character well enough to bring him or her to life, we don't have to know where the character came from.

Since most of this character history is told through flashbacks, and since you bring your present story to a halt whenever you start a flashback, it doesn't take many flashbacks to make your present-day story hard to follow. So if you find your story too heavily burdened with the past, consider letting some of the past go. The characterization you draw from the flashback may not be needed, or you may be able to find a way to bring it out in the present.

We recently worked on a book about a superficially happy man in his early forties who begins to explore his past after his second marriage fails. He starts out in an attempt to win his ex-wife back and in the end discovers that several people around him, including his closest friends, are not who he thought they were. The story of the hero's past, which included a bizarrely abusive mother, was critical to the plot, and the author brought it out in a series of very well-written flashbacks.

The problem was that the author gave us flashbacks of the ex-wife's past, of the hero's father's childhood, and of the life of some of the hero's childhood friends. In the middle of the book, the author included six chapters in a row that were made up entirely of flashbacks with a paragraph or two at the beginning and end to give the flashback a frame—the hero's present life simply disappeared for more than a hundred pages. We suggested that the author cut all but the most essential flashbacks and let us get to know his characters in the present, rather than in the past.

So how do you go about establishing a character gradually

and unobtrusively? The art of establishing a character is a large enough topic to make a book in itself, but there are some techniques that fall within the area of fiction mechanics. You can have one character characterized by another character instead of by the author. Rather than writing, "Cuthbert was not the sort of person whom others were drawn to immediately," you can simply have one of your characters say, "Like most people, I disliked Cuthbert on first sight."

Another unobtrusive way to develop a character is to write not about the character directly but about other matters in that character's voice. This amounts to your giving us your character's views of the world rather than your views of your character. Consider the opening paragraph of Graham Greene's *Monsignor Quixote*:

> It happened this way. Father Quixote had ordered his solitary lunch from his housekeeper and set off to buy wine at a local cooperative eight kilometers away from El Toboso on the main road to Valencia. It was a day when the heat stood and quivered on the dry fields, and there was no air conditioning in the little Seat 600 he had bought, already second hand, eight years before. As he drove he thought sadly of the day when he would have to find a new car. A dog's years can be multiplied by seven to equal a man's, and by that calculation his car would still be in early middle age, but he noticed how already his parishioners began to regard his Seat as almost senile. "You can't trust it, Don Quixote," they would warn him, and he could only reply, "It has been with me through many bad days, and I pray God that it may survive me." So many of his prayers had remained unanswered that he had hopes that this one prayer of his had lodged all the time like wax in the Eternal ear.

This characterization is not particularly gradual. We have known Father Quixote for all of one paragraph, but by its end we know quite a lot about him, his circumstances, his turn of mind, his personality, his sense of humor. Notice that Greene says absolutely nothing about Quixote himself. He talks about the priest's car, his parishioners, his prayer life, not about his character. But because we get all of this information from Quixote's point of view, the priest is there before us.

And finally, you can develop your character through dialogue and beats. We'll cover both of these topics in considerable detail later. But for now, if you want to learn who someone really is, watch what they say and do. And if you want your readers to get a feel for who your characters really are, then do it through dialogue and action.

Everything we've said about characterization applies to exposition as well. In fact, some types of exposition—such as scene setting or background—are really characterization except that what's being characterized is a location or a family rather than a person. Background, backstory (what happened before the story begins), the information your readers need in order to follow and appreciate your plot, should all be brought out as unobtrusively as possible.

When you give your readers all of your exposition all at once—when you devote three pages to the history of Milwaukee before your first scene, for instance—you run the risk of feeding them more information than they can absorb. And unless you're John le Carré, you can't get by with forcing readers to flip pages back and forth in order to follow your story. You also run the risk of lecturing your readers. A good rule of thumb is to give your readers only as much background information, or history, or characterization, as they need at any given time.

The theory and practice of circumventing burglar alarms was a major part of the plot in a police procedural we edited recently. In the first draft, the author included nearly an entire chapter on how various types of burglar alarms work and how they can be defeated—which, of course, effectively stopped his story short while he delivered a lecture. In his second draft he worked the same information in at various places throughout the book, giving readers just as much burglar-alarm theory as they needed to know at any given time.

The most obtrusive type of exposition is, of course, long discourses in the narrative voice. As you'll remember from the first chapter, these blocks of what is essentially nonfiction can usually be converted into immediate scenes. But just because exposition takes place in a scene doesn't necessarily mean it's unobtrusive. A few decades ago most stage plays opened with what they called "a feather duster." The maid (carrying a feather duster) would walk on the stage and answer a conveniently placed telephone:

> Hello? . . . No, Master Reginald isn't here. He and Mistress Elmira went to the airport to pick up his long-lost brother Zack, who disappeared twenty years ago with half the family fortune and has now been found living in the Andes. . . . What? No, young Master Roderick isn't here either. He and his young lady, Faith Hubberthwait-Jones, have gone off to see his solicitor about the possibility of opening the trust fund left to him by Great-Uncle Fornsby . . . . Yes, she is Lord Hubberthwait-Jones's daughter—a fine old family, but not a penny to their name . . . . No, I'm afraid Blump, the groundskeeper, isn't here either. He is running the prize hound, Artaxerxes, in the Bridgeton Meet in hopes of winning enough to cover his gambling debts. . . . Yes, thank you, I'll tell them you called.

Technically this sort of thing is dialogue, but it doesn't really sound like anything anyone on this planet, in this century, would actually say. It *is* possible to get exposition across unobtrusively through dialogue, but when your characters start discussing matters solely for the sake of informing your readers, the exposition tends to get in the way of believable characterization. So be on the lookout for places where your dialogue is actually exposition in disguise.

The same holds true for interior monologue. We once worked on a historical mystery set in a convent in sixteenth-century Spain. At one point, the main character simply sat in her room and pondered such everyday details of convent life as why the sisters were given the rooms they occupied. Technically it was interior monologue, but it was also out of character—people simply don't sit around and think about mundane details of life. In the author's next draft a new sister arrived at the convent and complained that her room was too small, and the information came out naturally through a scene.

The passage that follows (taken from a novel we edited a few years ago) illustrates just how unobtrusive exposition can get—and how enjoyable it can be for the reader. The point of view is that of a church organist, sitting at her console and watching mourners file in for a funeral service:

> She might've known Fitzhugh Jordan would be there. Some nerve, after all he did to keep that girl from coming home for Christmas. And just look at him, slipping into that pew beside his daddy, sweet as Gabriel blowing his horn. She was surprised Peter Griffith would let him in the church; then again, she wasn't, considering.
>
> Peter and Melinda Griffith were the last ones. And not a minute too soon. Mary Lou was about to run out of music and have to repeat herself.
>
> Peter walked right close to Melinda, though there could've been a wall of glass between them for all the contact they made. But Mary Lou had to admit they made a handsome couple—Peter tall and dark like an Italian movie star, Melinda blond and sweet-looking, though looks do lie.
>
> Melinda looked *wounded*, that was the only word for it. Hands fluttering, eyes glancing off people's faces like moths off a window.
>
> The two of them followed Fitzhugh into the family pew, which meant Mary Lou could finally wind down.
>
> She thought she'd close with "Abide with Me."

Notice how much of the recent history of the Jordan family surfaces in these paragraphs. Fitzhugh's opposition to "that girl" (whose identity is clear in the context), Peter and Melinda's lost love, Melinda's pain . . . . And it all comes to the reader through Mary Lou's interior monologue. Yet Mary Lou is such a credible character, and this material is so much *in* character, that none of this exposition feels like exposition. We take in the information not just painlessly but with real pleasure.

Again, just to prove that other people besides editors notice cumbersome exposition, here is a quote from Robert Stuart Nathan's review of Victor O'Reilly's *Games of the Hangman*:

> The novel's other sins include vast passages of irrelevant exposition; people ignorant of common facts, such as the police official who says the dead boy was "from a place called Bern," only to have Hugo obligingly respond, "It's the Swiss capital"; and characters awkwardly informing each other of things they already know, solely for the reader's benefit, as when one character asks, "Do you know the story of the original Alibe?" and Hugo replies, "Remind me."

What about exposition that provides necessary information or desirable atmosphere about the setting for a scene to come? "Feelings are bound up in place," Eudora Welty says in *The Eye of the Story*. "Location is the crossroads of circumstance, the proving ground of 'What happened? Who's here? Who's coming?'" Experienced novelists often begin a scene or chapter with a description of the setting for the scene about to come. If this exposition is skillful enough, the reader is likely to feel put on—perhaps even in—the scene.

A master at unobtrusive exposition is C. J. Cherryh, a novelist who writes science fiction and fantasy. In her Chanur books she drops her readers into the middle of what amounts to a war between several alien species triggered by the discovery of humanity. The main character is an alien, many of the other characters are *very* alien (one minor character is a sort of methane-breathing snake/starfish who talks in seven-part matrices and sometimes gives birth during a conversation), the technology is futuristic, the sociology is complex, and the interspecies intrigues are Byzantine. And the author explains *nothing*—aside from the index, there is not a single paragraph of outright exposition in the four books that comprise the series.

This sink-or-swim approach may be a little extreme, and

some readers are doubtless left behind by the intricacies of Cherryh's alien politics and interstellar trade routes. But readers who stick with the books become deeply—even passionately—involved in them. By never explaining her situations, by trusting her readers to keep up with her, Cherryh pays her readers the compliment of assuming them to be intelligent.

And that's a compliment any author would do well to pass along.

CHECKLIST

•Look back over a scene or chapter that introduces one or more characters. How much time, if any, have you spent describing the new characters' character? Are you telling us about characteristics that will later show up in dialogue and action?

•How about character histories? How many of your characters' childhoods have you developed in detail? Can some of these life stories be cut?

•What information (technical details, characters' past histories, backgrounds on locations or families) do your readers need in order to understand your story? At what point in the story do they need to know it?

•How are you getting this information across to your readers? Have you given it to them all at once through a short author-to-reader lecture (see exercise B)?

•If the exposition comes out through dialogue, is it through dialogue your characters would actually speak even if your readers didn't have to know the information? In other words, does the dialogue exist only to put the information across?

•If the exposition is through interior monologue, would your characters actually think these thoughts if your readers didn't have to know the information?

EXERCISES

A. *How would you develop the following character through a series of scenes? (Keep in mind that the scenes don't have to be consecutive, and some of the material need not be included at all.)*

Maggie had reached the cusp of her childhood, that gray area between girl and woman when she could be either, neither, or both almost at will. There had not been (and probably would not be) a lonelier time in her life. She could no longer associate with children, whose interests now bored her. But she wasn't comfortable with adults, for she still carried the energy of a child and could not slow herself down to match their pace.

And so she found herself trapped between the banal and the dull, trying to shape her life with only the help of her contemporaries, who were as adrift as she was. Given all this, was it any wonder she sometimes seemed, well, exasperated to her parents?

B. *Now try the same thing with a passage of exposition.*

The county had changed over the years. It had all started with the George Washington Bridge, which finally put the west side of the Hudson within commuting distance of New York City without the bother of trains and ferries. Then had come the Tappan Zee

Bridge, a second artery running right through the heart of the county. It was only a matter of time before the family farms were turned into developments and the little two-lane roads became four-lane highways.

Fred could remember when Nanuet only had one traffic light. Now it had a string of twelve of them on Route 59 alone, mostly in front of the mall. (The mall!) And Route 59 itself was well on its way to becoming a continuous string of malls and shopping centers, all the way from Nyack to Suffern and beyond. It had reached the point where shoppers outnumbered residents three to one on a busy day.

....

POINT OF VIEW

"Want some buttermilk?" July asked, going to the crock.

"No, sir," Joe said. He hated buttermilk, but July loved it so that he always asked anyway.

"You ask him that every night," Elmira said from the edge of the loft. It irritated her that July came home and did exactly the same things day after day.

"Stop asking him," she said sharply. "Let him get his own buttermilk if he wants any. It's been four months now and he ain't drunk a drop—looks like you'd let it go."

She spoke with a heat that surprised July. Elmira could get angry about almost anything, it seemed. Why would it matter if he invited the boy to have a drink of buttermilk? All he had to do was say no, which he had.

Larry McMurtry's *Lonesome Dove* is a powerfully written book, yet some readers find it hard to get involved in the story, in part because of passages like the above. The characters are clear, the dialogue has an authentic feel. But in the second paragraph we're seeing the scene as Joe sees it, in the third we've switched to Elmira, and in the last paragraph we've switched again, to July. Although some writing books distinguish as many as twenty-six different types of point of view, there are really only three basic approaches: first person, third person, and omniscient. The first person is the "I" voice, where all the narration is written as if the narrator were speaking directly to the readers. ("I knew as soon as I entered the room that something was wrong, but it was a few seconds before I realized what it was—the stuffed moose was missing.") Note that the narrator is one of the characters, not the author as in the omniscient point of view.

The first person point of view has a number of advantages, the main one being that it gives your readers a great deal of intimacy with your viewpoint character. When you are writing from the "I" perspective, your main character quite literally invites your readers into his or her head and shows them the world through his or her eyes. Consider the following example, adapted from a submission to one of our workshops:

> I never thought I'd see the day when I was thankful for the oak.
>
> I certainly wasn't thankful this last autumn when I stood with my rake in the middle of the scraggly patches of grass that pass for the front yard and cursed the leaves that, I swear, multiply on their way to the ground. And come autumn, I'll probably stand and curse the tree again.
>
> But for now, when it seems the dog days have come to stay forever, when the sun'd bake anyone fool enough to venture off his porch and onto the street—well, that tree is a positive comfort.

Or consider the opening of Andrew Greeley's *God Game*:

> It was Nathan's fault that I became God.
> It is, as I would learn, hell to be God.
> Nathan, to begin with, is as close to a genius as anyone I ever

expect to know. If this story has any moral at all, it is that you should stay away from geniuses.

It was in his role as impresario of software that he made me God. He's not a programmer but rather an interfacer, a software consumer who can talk Cobol or Pascal or whatever languages the programmers think in these days and tell them what we folks who don't know a bit from a byte need in the way of data-analysis packages.

He's also a fiction addict, which enables him to interface between the programmers and the fiction addicts of the world. That's how my troubles started.

Of course, in order to write from the first person point of view, you have to be able to create a character strong enough and interesting enough to keep your readers going for an entire novel—yet not so eccentric or bizarre that your readers feel trapped inside his or her head. And what you gain in intimacy with the first person, you lose in perspective. You can't write about anything your main character couldn't know, which means you have to have your main character on the spot whenever you want to write an immediate scene.

The first person point of view limits your perspective in another way as well. When you write your entire novel from one point of view, your readers really only get to know one character directly. Everyone else is filtered through your viewpoint character. One way around this is to write in the first person from several different viewpoints with different scenes done from inside the heads of different characters, a technique that can be highly effective in the hands of an experienced novelist. Sol Stein's novels often use it—over the course of a recent one, *The Best Revenge*, first-person sections are written from the points of view of six different characters. And Mary Gordon devotes the last section in *The Company of Women* to first-person accounts by all the major characters in turn.

The omniscient point of view could almost be considered the opposite of the first person. Instead of being written from inside the head of one of your characters, a scene in the omni-

"The Rapid Express man is here with your manuscript. He says you have too many points of view from too many characters. He says all these jumps are distracting, to say the least."

scient point of view is not written from inside anyone's head. You may think of omniscient narration as a nineteenth-century technique ("It was the best of times, it was the worst of times." or "Happy families are all alike. But every unhappy family is unhappy in a different way."). And it's true that the omniscient point of view reached its most extreme form in nineteenth-century novels such as George Eliot's *Middlemarch*, in which it was not uncommon for the author to address the reader directly:

> If you want to know more particularly how Mary looked, ten to one you will see a face like hers in the crowded street tomorrow, if you are there on the watch: she will not be among those daughters of Zion who are haughty, and walk with stretched-out necks and wanton eyes, mincing as they go. Let all those pass, and fix your eyes on some small plump brownish person of firm but quiet carriage, who looks about her, but does not suppose that anybody is looking at her.

You're unlikely to want to go as far as this—it's difficult to maintain authorial transparency when you're having a chat with your readers—but the omniscient point of view in its milder forms does have its advantages. And a number of successful modern authors, from Larry McMurtry and Joyce Carol Oates to Kurt Vonnegut and Faye Weldon, have written powerful novels using the omniscient point of view.

Consider these paragraphs, from R. F. Delderfield's *The Dreaming Suburb*:

> In the spring of 1947 the bulldozers moved down the cart-track beside Number Seventeen and deployed across the meadow to the fringe of Manor Wood. The bulldozers ravaged the Avenue and despoiled its memories. In the first week they clawed down the tiny greenhouse where Esme first kissed Elaine, and Elaine's father, Edgar, had tended his hyacinths and planned to abandon his family; it was not long before concrete mixers were set up on the very spot where Judy Carver had pledged her soul to Esme Fraser and later, when the first Dorniers droned overhead, Elaine Frith had lain with her Polish lover in the long, parched grass . . .

Notice how easy the omniscient point of view makes it to introduce information—such as the neighborhood's being torn down—that your readers may need to know but you may find it hard to work into a scene. All narrative summary is written in the omniscient point of view, almost by definition.

But also notice that what you gain in perspective you may lose in intimacy. Take a look at the workshop passage we quoted earlier, rewritten into the omniscient narrative voice:

> In small South Carolina towns, most houses are built in the shadow of tall trees. Each autumn, the children charged with yard care curse the leaves that seem to multiply on their way to the ground. But in mid-afternoon during the dog days of August, when the blazing sun takes possession of the streets and bakes anyone who dares to challenge it, entire families retreat to their front porches, there to await whatever stray breezes happen by in the shade of those same trees.
>
> One such tree, a tall oak, stood in the front yard of the house Coral Blake rented from a man who had long ago moved his family north. The lush expanse of the oak belied the barren nature of the surrounding yard, where little grew except sparse clumps of grass, random weeds, and a scraggly pair of hydrangea bushes—pale blue instead of violet.

This passage contains all the information of the previous version but it lacks the warmth, the sense of what it actually feels like to sit under an old oak tree in the dog days of summer.

The third person point of view is a compromise between the first person and omniscient, providing you with a mixture of perspective and intimacy. Take a look at the workshop example, rewritten one final time:

> Coral Blake mopped the sweat out of her eyes and looked up at the dusty green underside of the oak. The dog days of August had come to stay, it seemed, and like most of the rest of Greeleyville, South Carolina, she sought refuge from the sun on her front porch under the oak.
>
> Her children hated that tree. Every fall she'd chase them out to the scraggly front yard with a rake, and every fall she'd watch them curse the leaves that seemed to multiply as they fell. But

now, with her head leaning back against the cool metal of the glider, the tree seemed like a blessing.

Although the narrative voice is not as strong as in the first-person version, we still get an idea of what it feels like to be Coral Blake on a hot summer afternoon. But with the third person point of view, you can move from character to character more easily than with the first person. This allows your readers to see your story from different perspectives.

In the first chapter, we talked about how you construct immediate scenes. A distinguishing feature of most scenes is that they are written in the third person from a single point of view. Again, this may be the effect of decades of movies and television—readers now see stories from what is, in effect, the camera's point of view. (Movies with a narrative voiceover, such as the *film noir* movies made in the forties and fifties, manage to achieve something close to the first-person point of view, but these films are the exception.) As a result, the third person point of view is the one most authors choose.

And the problem you are most likely to have with the third person is keeping the point of view consistent throughout each of your scenes. You have to decide which character you are going to use to view the scene and then describe only what that character would see and hear. If the murder weapon has been hidden behind the couch and your viewpoint character can't see it, you don't mention it. All your descriptions, all your observations, all your interior monologue will belong to the same viewpoint character.

Consider the following example from a manuscript by a talented first novelist:

> [Markey has just informed Mrs. Blake that her son is dead]
> "What happened?" She was standing under the archway to the living room, staring at him.
> Markey looked up. Apparently she was going to be trouble.
> "He was in a kayak," he said.

"A kayak. I see." She stepped back into the room. "Then he drowned?"

"Yes, Mrs. Blake, we assume so."

"What do you mean you assume so?" Her voice began to rise. "How can you stand there and tell me you assume so. Who are you?"

"Clayton Markey, ma'am."

She could feel his discomfort at being on the other side of a question.

The second paragraph in this example ("Apparently she was going . . .") is clearly from Markey's point of view. But by the last paragraph we have moved into Mrs. Blake's head ("She could feel his discomfort . . ."). The transition from one point of view to the other is gradual, with several paragraphs of dialogue between. But still, the readers have adjusted to being in Markey's head (they were in his head for most of the previous page), so the shift to Mrs. Blake's head is jarring even though it's not abrupt. Enough of these shifts, and readers lose their involvement in the story.

Which is a good reason to be wary of writing in the omniscient point of view unless you're not only a very gifted writer but also a very experienced one. Maintaining a truly omniscient point of view throughout an entire novel is, to say the least, tricky. Most authors eventually start dipping into the heads of various characters over the course of a scene—writing from the third person point of view but with different viewpoint characters.

Some authors get into trouble with their point of view because they are trying to track the emotions of everyone involved in the scene. After all, the easiest way to show how someone feels is through interior monologue—get into his or her head and tell your readers what's there. So when you have several characters in a scene, there's an understandable temptation to simply write interior monologues for all of them.

And it's a temptation we hope you'll resist. For one thing, shifting the point of view back and forth is likely to do more damage to the flow of the scene than the various viewpoints are worth. (As we said, your readers adjust to being in someone's head—they assume that they are seeing the scene through that character's eyes. So when you shift to another character, you throw them off their stride, even if just for a moment.) For another, using interior monologue to show your character's reactions is just one step away from telling. It is far more effective to stick with a single point of view and *show* us how your other characters feel through their dialogue and actions.

Sometimes an author will jump from character to character as a way of working in more information than one character could possibly take in. In an earlier scene from the manuscript quoted above, the author wrote alternating paragraphs from the point of view of Mrs. Blake (in the shower) and of Markey (walking through her building's lobby and riding the elevator to her floor). The author was using this crosscutting technique to build suspense about Markey's approach, a technique that might have worked well—only the jumps back and forth created so much confusion that the tension was undermined.

Or take another example, this one from pages submitted at one of the company's workshops. A group of men led by Elwood are (for reasons we can't get into now) relandscaping the yard of a movie mogul, Zoltan Diesel, without his knowledge. Harley, one of the men, is perched on a telephone pole outside of Diesel's estate (and presumably out of sight) to act as a lookout in case Diesel returns. Ford is an acquaintance of Diesel's who shows up unexpectedly.

"What's going on?" Harley switched the walkie-talkie back on.

Elwood leaned back on the belt that held him high in the tree and yelled to Ford above the noise of the saws. "Mister, I can't be responsible for your car, you leave it there. We got branches falling all over the place."

"Who's there?" Harley said over the walkie-talkie. "Elwood, what's going on?"

"If we scratch that car," Stilton said, "our insurance don't cover it."

"Typical Diesel performance," Ford said. "Total disregard of anybody else's time. Whatever's going on, he can solve it." Ford gave a final puzzled look, got in the car—opening the door this time—and pulled out.

"Jesus," said Bart, "why'd you take a chance talking to him?"

"Because if he stayed here, sooner or later he'd recognize one of us," Elwood said. "And we wouldn't be able to get out if he did. The Beverly Hills cops are fast."

This is a well-written scene with clear character voices and vivid details, but the author is trying to capture too many things at the same time: Harley's confusion, Stilton's self-assurance, Ford's disgust. In the process she has muddied the point of view and reduced the reader's involvement in the scene. (There are at least two point of view shifts—finding them is left as an exercise for the reader.)

So, what happens when you *have* to shift your point of view for the sake of the plot—if, say, you are writing from Inspector Hendricks' point of view and want to establish that Jeeves the Butler is nervous without letting Hendricks know? How do you change the point of view without jerking your readers around? It's quite simple: end the current scene, insert a linespace, and start a new scene from the new point of view you need. The linespace will prepare your readers for a shift (in time, place, or point of view), so the shift won't catch them by surprise.

The example with Elwood and company (above) could be written as follows:

Harley switched the walkie-talkie back on and slapped it to his ear. "What's going on?"

He could hear Stilton yelling above the noise of the saws. "Mister, I can't be responsible for your car, you leave it there. We got branches falling all over the place."

"Who's there?" Harley said. "Elwood, what's happening?"

Elwood leaned back on the belt and stared at Ford below him.

"Mister, if we scratch that car," he said, "our insurance don't cover it."

"Typical Diesel performance," Ford yelled back. "Total disregard of anybody else's time. Whatever's going on, he can solve it."

He threw Elwood a final puzzled look, then got in the car—opening the door this time—and pulled out.

"Jesus," Bart said once he was gone, "why'd you take a chance talking to him?"

"Because if he stayed here, sooner or later he'd recognize one of us," Elwood said. "And we wouldn't be able to get out if he did. The Beverly Hills cops are fast."

Here there are only two points of view—Harley's (which includes only what he would hear through the walkie-talkie) and Elwood's (which includes only what he would see from the top of the tree). And the linespace clearly marks the dividing line between them. Note that a shift in the point of view falls between two consecutive lines of dialogue—a point of view shift doesn't necessarily mean a break in time.

Now take a look at this example from *Touch*, by Elmore Leonard:

[Lynn is being interviewed by a pushy talk show host. Juvenal is watching from offstage.]

"Hey, it's beautiful," Howard said. "You're young, you're in love. Heck, then what's wrong with sleeping together?" He paused. "Unless you're ashamed to admit it, feel it's something dirty, obscene." Howard frowned. "If you're in love, why would you feel guilty about sleeping together?"

"I *don't* feel guilty. I haven't said anything about . . . our relationship." The son of a bitch, he was even worse than she thought.

"You haven't denied anything either. Hey, I'm not judging. If you're having an affair with him, that's your business—"

"—but if you bring it on my show then it becomes *my* business because, honey, I can talk to you about anything I want—" Juvenal heard Howard say, as he was trying to hear what August was telling him through his clenched teeth, painfully, with a great effort.

Here Leonard breaks the scene and shifts the point of view in the middle of a line of dialogue, yet the shift is perfectly clear, and the sharp break adds to the tension of an already tense scene.

It's usually a good idea to establish the point of view in the first paragraph of a scene—even the first sentence—in order to orient the reader. "Mortimer stretched out in the hammock, a novel, unread, propped open on his chest, lemonade on the lawn beside him, hat pulled over his eyes. Everything was in place for a perfect day." "Blanche stared at the rows upon rows of identical cubicles that made up her office and decided to pack it in and move to Montana." "Letitia was in the sitting room when she heard the first shots." When you make the point of view clear at the beginning of a scene you get your readers involved early—and your scene off to a quick, sharp start.

The only exception—and just about the only time it's effective to mix points of view in a scene—is to start out in omniscient narration and then ease into a specific third-person point of view. In effect, you can perform the literary equivalent of a camera moving from a long shot to gradually close the distance from the actor. In *The Jesuit* John Gallahue uses this technique simply and very effectively:

One morning in 1931, in early June, the pious routine of the rector of a sleepy seminary in Maryland was spectacularly interrupted. A young priest from the office of the Apostolic Delegate in Washington, D.C., personally delivered a sealed message from Rome to the Superior of the House. He did not wait for a reply; indeed, as he informed the rector of the seminary, he had no knowledge whatsoever of the contents. Saying no more, the priest departed, leaving Father Dillon to peruse the brief message.

We read the message—demanding extraordinary treatment of a young scholastic named Ulanov—along with Father Dillon, at which point the camera moves in closer, to third-person point of view though still at some distance:

> Father Dillon read the telegram three or four times. Finally, he delegated one of his seminarians to fetch his confidential house consultant—Father Sullivan, a former rector now eighty years old. Together, they tried to comprehend the import of this extraordinary communication.

The two men discuss the appointment, what it may mean, and Dillon's forebodings—mostly dialogue, the snippets of narration all third person with an ever-tightening focus on Dillon. By the time the increasingly tense scene ends, the reader is firmly in Dillon's head and likely to be sharing his uneasiness about Ulanov:

> The rector was still left with his power of decision, and he meant to exercise it. It wasn't that he found anything bad in the young man. No, that would represent a loss of balance, and if there was one virtue the rector prided himself on possessing it was perspective. He simply sensed in the young Jesuit an empty spot. But even that wouldn't have mattered much if Rome hadn't been so insistent on his promotion.

The novel is told from the third-person point of view of various characters, the tightening-focus technique used time and again to increasingly suspenseful effect. Father Dillon's misgivings turn out to be so justified that the reader remembers them hundreds of pages later—and wishes passionately that Dillon's judgment had prevailed over Rome's.

Up until now we've been talking about point of view as an essentially mechanical matter—you choose a particular character to perceive a given scene and write only what your viewpoint character would see or hear. But point of view can also be understood in a more subtle stylistic sense, one closer to art than craft: you describe only what your viewpoint character would see—and only in terms your viewpoint character would use. In other words you not only show the world through your viewpoint character's eyes, you show the world through his or her mind. As we mentioned in the last chapter, this is a wonderfully unobtrusive way to create a character. When you do it right, the third person point of view can become almost as intimate as the first, and the first person can become mesmerizing.

Billy Bittinger uses this technique to characterize her heroine with enviable unobtrusiveness and a delightful comic sensibility in the opening paragraphs of *The Good Time Gospel Boys*:

> Every time the Good Time Gospel Quartet came to town, Lucille Byrd got laid. Since Lucille was six feet tall and weighed three hundred pounds buck naked, and since the Good Time Gospel Quartet only came once a year, a sultry weekend in August, once a year was plenty and at that it took all four of the Gospel Boys to take care of her. She gave in return, however. Each year, when the quartet rolled in, they parked their bus behind the Holy Roller church and went directly into the sanctuary to make sure the piano was halfway in tune. As soon as she spotted the bus from where she was waiting at the general store across the street, Lucille would run right over to the church to greet them, and then that night she'd perform with them. She would sing, Lord, how she would sing.

We never hear a word about Lucille's character, yet the description of her relation to the quartet gives us a sharp sense of who she is. Ms. Bittinger has characterized her heroine simply by letting us into her head.

William Faulkner was a master at this technique. If you've ever read *The Sound and The Fury* or *As I Lay Dying*, you can open them at random and, within a paragraph or two, know which character's head you're in. Faulkner has given each of his characters such a distinctive interior voice that, as you read, you really feel you are seeing the world through the eyes of a desperate young woman or an insensitive middle-aged man. It's a powerful technique when it's done well.

Sol Stein is a contemporary author who uses the technique effectively. Consider these two paragraphs from *The Best Revenge*, in which two different characters talk about their businesses:

> And so within a year, I was making out of metal a leaf so real-looking an onlooker could fool himself for half a second into believing it was from a tree. And within two years, as anyone who knew me could have predicted, I had parted company with Zalatnick and set up a shop in Chicago.
>
> Twice I lent money to Golub, a beer distributor on Long Island. The second time, when it's due he twiddles me. We have a big argument in his office, he calls the cops to throw me out, you believe that? Worse, he throws a lawsuit at me for three times what I lent him, on the grounds that I am interfering with his business.

Each passage has its own rhythm and voice—the first slow and easygoing, the second sharp and driving—and so the two paragraphs draw the readers, almost subconsciously, into two very different minds. Writing in a character's voice puts your readers intimately in touch with your characters.

Of course, there are times when you don't want your readers to get too intimate with your characters. If your main character is a psychotic killer, you may want to write his scenes in the third person using a more neutral, distant voice—after all, you want to engage your readers, not drive them to distraction. But more often than not you want your readers to be drawn in by a character, to share his or her concerns, to see if only for an instant the world the way he or she sees it. Placing your readers firmly in one character's head—and staying there—can be a remarkably effective way to accomplish this.

CHECKLIST

• Which point of view are you using and why? How much intimacy do you want to create between your readers and your characters? Which point of view will make it easiest for you to unfold your story?

• If you're writing in the first person, how reader-friendly is your viewpoint character? Is it someone you would want to spend three or four hundred pages with?

• If you're writing from the third person, take a look at each scene. Whose head are you in? Do you stay in that head for the length of the scene?

• How soon do you establish the point of view? Where in the scene is the first line that tells your readers unambiguously whose head they are in?

• Are you writing your scenes in your characters' voices, describing their surroundings in terms they would use? Do you want to write in your characters' voices, or do you want something more neutral, more distant, more unobtrusive?

EXERCISES
Spot the point of view problems:

A. Susan heard the key in the lockbox and then a second key in the front door. She grabbed Ed by the arm.

"My God, I forgot, it's the realtors."

He looked around the living room, at the papers strewn on the couch, the mail piled on the coffee table. He remembered the two days' worth of dishes in the kitchen sink. "What, you mean today? Now? With people?"

They had no time to lose. "You take the kitchen, I'll handle here."

Susan began gathering papers and shoving them in the fire-

POINT OF VIEW • 45

place while Ed made a dash for the kitchen. Once there, he grabbed the dishpan and began stacking things in it as quietly as he could. He then hoisted the overflowing pan out of the sink and kicked open the cupboard.

No, they would look in the cupboard. Where then, the refrigerator? Behind the furnace in the basement?

He ducked out the back door just as Susan backed into the kitchen just in front of the realtor and an earnest young couple.

"You're sure you wouldn't like to tour the upstairs first?" she asked.

"No, actually, I'd like to see the basement," the young man said. "You see, I'm thinking of setting up a shop in my home, and I need to know if there's enough space."

"Oh, very well."

Ed came back through the living room just as the couple disappeared down the steps.

"Okay, where are the dishes?" Susan said.

"Trunk of the car."

B. A battered New York cab pulled over to the curb and

Lance climbed in. The cabbie was a slight, withdrawn man who wasn't much given to conversation. This was fine with Lance, who buried himself in the *Times* as the cab wound its way north through the traffic choking the Park Avenue tunnel.

Finally the cab pulled up to Grand Central Terminal. Lance handed the cabbie a ten and disappeared into the crowd.

C. Take a sample scene of, say, an eight-year-old boy named Mitch in school on a Thursday afternoon at the moment he looks out the window and realizes that the first snowfall of the year has begun. Write this scene from the first person, third person, and omniscient points of view.

D. Remember Maggie from the last chapter? Well, let's say her mother Eloise (a stately, genteel, and perhaps slightly dull woman) is taking her Christmas shopping for her younger brother, Mitch. Maggie came along reluctantly and wants to get back home as quickly as possible so she can field a phone call from Brad.

Write two versions of this little scene, one from Maggie's point of view and the other from her mother's. Try to capture the differences in their personalities in the way you describe the world around them. In other words, write the same scene in two different character voices.

CHAPTER 4

....

DIALOGUE MECHANICS

Mr. [Robert] Ludlum has other peculiarities. For example, he hates the "he said" locution and avoids it as much as possible. Characters in *The Bourne Ultimatum* seldom "say" anything. Instead, they cry, interject, interrupt, muse, state, counter, conclude, mumble, whisper (Mr. Ludlum is great on whispers), intone, roar, exclaim, fume, explode, mutter. There is one especially unforgettable tautology: "'I repeat,' repeated Alex."

The book may sell in the billions, but it's still junk.

—Newgate Callender, in *The New York Times Book Review*

What's the first thing acquisitions editors look for when they begin reading a fiction submission? Several editors we know have answered that question the same way: "The first thing I do is find a scene with some dialogue. If the dialogue doesn't work, the manuscript gets bounced. If it's good, I start reading."

If you're like most authors you probably find that writing dialogue takes more thought than writing narration or action.

Your characters come alive—or fail to—when they speak, and it's no easy matter to put just the right words in their mouths.

And because it's such hard work, generations of writers have developed mechanical tricks to save them the trouble of writing dialogue that effectively conveys character and emotion—techniques to prop up shaky dialogue, or to paper over holes and make second-rate dialogue serviceable without a lot of effort. Not surprisingly these are the very tricks to avoid if you want your dialogue to read like the work of a professional instead of an amateur or a hack.

Once you learn to spot these creaky mechanics, all you have to do is stop using them. And once you stop, you may find that your dialogue—standing on its own—is a lot stronger than you thought it was when you wrote it. (All those unnecessary supports you set up around it just made it *look* weak.) And should you find that your dialogue doesn't stand on its own, then at least you'll know where your next writing task lies.

Imagine you're at a play. It's the middle of the first act, you're getting to know the characters, and you're getting really involved in the drama they're acting out. Suddenly the playwright runs out on the stage and yells, "Do you see what's happening here? Do you see how her coldness is behind his infidelity? Have you noticed the way his womanizing has undermined her self-confidence? Do you get it?"

You get it, of course, and you feel patronized. You're an intelligent theatergoer, and what's happening on the stage is clear enough. You don't need the author to explain it to you.

This is exactly what happens when you explain your dialogue to your readers. Consider the following:

"You can't be serious," she said in astonishment.

If you're like most novelists or short-story authors, you write sentences like these almost without thinking. What could be easier than to simply tell the readers how a character feels? If she is astonished, you just say so—it saves all sorts of time and trouble.

It's also lazy writing. When your dialogue is well written, describing your characters' emotions to your readers is just as patronizing as a playwright running onto the stage and yelling at the audience. "You can't be serious" conveys astonishment—no explanation is needed. And when you explain dialogue that needs no explanation, you are writing down to your readers, a sure-fire way to turn them off. The theatergoer might or might not walk out of a theater when the playwright runs on stage; the reader who feels patronized will almost certainly close the book. Once again, Resist the Urge to Explain (R.U.E.).

And if your dialogue isn't well written—if it needs the explanations to convey the emotions—then the explanations really won't help. Say you'd written:

"I find that difficult to accept," she said in astonishment.

Here the explanation does let your readers know that your character is astonished. But you don't want them to know the fact, you want them to feel the emotion. You want your readers to be as astonished as she is, and the only way to do that is to have her say something your readers can imagine themselves saying when they're astonished. "I find that difficult to accept," doesn't quite do it.

And if you tell your readers she is astonished when her dialogue doesn't *show* astonishment, then you've created an uncomfortable tension between your dialogue and your explanation. Your dialogue says one thing; your explanation, something slightly different. True, your readers probably won't notice—the truth is, only editors and reviewers really notice these things. But your readers will be aware, perhaps subconsciously, that something is wrong. And that awareness will undermine their involvement in your book.

Think about it. There are as many different ways to be astonished (or angry or relieved or overjoyed) as there are people. The way we react under the influence of strong emotion is one of the things that makes us who we are. If you tell your readers your character is astonished, all they will know is that she is astonished. But if you show *how* she is astonished through her dialogue or through a beat, then your readers will know a little more about her. (She dropped the whisk, splattering meringue up the cupboard door. "You can't be serious.") It's showing and telling again, applied to dialogue.

"You can't be serious" also has a formality and a coldness about it—compared to, say, "You've got to be kidding," or "You pulling my chain, dude?" A character likely to say "You can't be serious" is also likely to be prim, or proper, maybe a little uptight. And if all of her dialogue conveys primness, then your readers will get to know her character without your ever having to describe her as "prim."

Think of it this way: Every time you insert an explanation into dialogue, you're cheating your readers of a little bit of one of your characters. Do it often enough, and none of your characters ever comes to life on the page.

Also, while most of your explanations will probably involve your characters' emotions, be on the lookout for those that explain the content of the dialogue:

> Percy burst into the zookeeper's office. Their callous mistreatment was killing the wombats and he wasn't going to stand for it.
>
> "Is something wrong, sir?" the zookeeper said.
>
> "Don't you realize you're killing those poor innocent creatures, you heartless fascist?" Percy yelled.

Again, if the dialogue already makes it clear, then you don't have to repeat it. Your readers will get it the first time. R.U.E.

Of course, dialogue explanations are rarely as obvious as this. More often they take the form of *-ly* adverbs, as in:

> "I'm afraid it's not going very well," he said grimly.
>
> "Keep scrubbing until you're finished," she said harshly.
>
> "I don't know, I can't seem to work up the steam to do anything at all," he said listlessly.

Perhaps it's a lack of confidence on the writer's part, perhaps it's simple laziness, or perhaps it's a misguided attempt to break up the monotony of using "said" all the time (more about that in a minute), but all too many fiction writers tend to pepper their dialogue with -*ly*s.

Which is a good reason to cut virtually every one you write. *Ly* adverbs almost always catch the author in the act of explaining dialogue—smuggling emotions into speaker attributions that belong in the dialogue itself. Again, if your dialogue doesn't need the props, putting the props in will make it seem weak even though it isn't.

There are a few exceptions to this principle—almost all of them adverbs that actually modify the verb "said," such as "he said softly" or "she said clearly." After all, you don't say something grimly in the same sense that you say something softly. The grimness comes across more by *what* you say and do— through word choice, body language, context—than by *how* you say it. Again, there are as many ways to be grim as there are people, and when you write "he said grimly," what you are really saying is, "he said this, and he felt pretty grim about it." You need to show the grimness, to show what your character does that makes him seem grim.

Besides, if you use them often enough, -*ly* adverbs begin to look like Tom Swifties—one-liners built around -*ly* adverbs that are named for the archetypal example: " 'Hurry up,' Tom said swiftly." Our favorite is, " 'Don't worry, the radiation level isn't very high,' Tom said glowingly."

For a final word on the subject, here's a quote from an interview with Gabriel Garcia Marquez:

To tighten his own writing, [Marquez] has eliminated adverbs, which in Spanish all have the ending -*mente* [the equivalent of -*ly*]. "Before *Chronicle of a Death Foretold*," he says, "there are many. In *Chronicle*, I think there is one. After that, in *Love* there are none. In Spanish, the adverb -*mente* is a very easy solution. But when you want to use -*mente* and look for another form, it [the other form] always is better. It has become so natural to me that I don't even notice anymore."

Unless your dialogue consists entirely of one character talking to himself or herself, you will need to include speaker attributions so your readers know who is saying what. Bear in mind that the *only* reason you need them is so your readers know who is saying what. Don't use speaker attributions as a way of slipping in explanations of your dialogue ("he growled," "she snapped"). As with all other types of explanations, either they're unnecessary ("I'm sorry," he apologized) or they are necessary but shouldn't be ("Do you consider that amusing?" she whined).

What this amounts to is your using the verb "said" almost without exception. ("I feel terrible about it," he said. "You always keep me waiting, you never call," she said.) Some authors get a little nervous when they see a long string of "saids" spreading over the pages—they hear the voices of their creative writing teachers telling them to strive for variety and originality in their verbs. So they write:

"Give it to me," she demanded.
"Here it is," he offered.
"Is it loaded?" she inquired.

Or, even worse:

"I hate to admit that," he grimaced.
"Come closer," she smiled.
"So you've changed your mind," he chuckled.

To use verbs like these last three for speaker attribution is to brand yourself an amateur—and to stick your character with an action that is physically impossible: no one outside of hack fiction has ever been able to grimace or smile or chuckle a sentence.

We're all in favor of choosing exactly the right verb for the

"Nobody is going to be the least bit upset, Leonard, if you simply insert another string of 'saids'...."

action, but when you're writing speaker attributions the right verb is nearly always "said." The reason those well-intentioned attempts at variety don't work is that verbs other than "said" tend to draw attention away from the dialogue. They jump out at the reader, make the reader aware, if only for a second, of the mechanics of writing. They draw attention to your technique, and a technique that distracts the reader is never a good idea. You want your readers to pay attention to your dialogue, not the means by which you get it to them.

"Said," on the other hand, isn't even read the way other verbs are read. It is, and should be, an almost purely mechanical device—more like a punctuation mark than a verb. It's absolutely transparent, and so is graceful and elegant. Which, actually, is another reason to avoid explanations and adverbs. Even when you use them with "said" (we said sternly), they tend to entangle your readers in your technique rather than leaving them free to concentrate on your dialogue.

There are other ways to keep your speaker attributions transparent. Don't open a paragraph of dialogue with the speaker attribution. Instead, start a paragraph with dialogue and place the speaker attribution at the first natural break in the first sentence. ("I don't know," he said, "I've always felt plungers were underrated as kitchen utensils.") This is an especially good idea when the paragraph is fairly long—the ear seems to require a break near the beginning.

Place the character's name or pronoun first in a speaker attribution ("Dave said"). Reversing the two ("said Dave"), though often done, is less professional. It has a slightly old-fashioned, first-grade-reader flavor ("Run, Spot, run," said Jane). After all, "said he" fell out of favor sometime during the Taft administration.

Decide how you are going to refer to a character and stick with it for at least the length of the scene. Don't use "Hubert said" on one page, "Mr. Winchester said," on the next, and "the old man said" on the third—if you do, your readers will have to stop reading long enough to figure out that the old man is Hubert. (This doesn't mean you have to stick with a single form of address for an entire novel, of course. If you want to show that your heroine is getting to know Mr. Winchester, for instance, you could have her refer to him as "Mr. Winchester" in chapter one, "Hubert" in chapter four, and "Hubie" in chapter ten.)

If it's clear from the dialogue who is speaking—if two characters are bantering back and forth, for instance—you can dispense with speaker attributions altogether. But don't ping-pong direct address in an attempt to get rid of speaker attributions:

> "I just don't believe he'd say that, Chet."
> "Well, Hortense, I may have heard wrong, but—"
> "Cut it out, Chet. Just cut it out."

This technique may serve you well once or twice, but it gets old very quickly. People just don't talk like that.

If you are still troubled by the number of "saids" in your dialogue, you can replace some of them with beats:

> "I'd never thought of that before." Roger walked over to the fridge and helped himself to a soda. "But I suppose a good coat of shellac really would work just as well, wouldn't it?"

Remember, so long as your readers can tell who is speaking, your speaker attributions have done just what they need to do.

Substituting beats for speaker attributions can come in especially handy when your dialogue involves three or more speakers. In this case, you have to let your readers know who is saying each line of dialogue. But if the lines are brief, you can wind up with a string of "saids" on the page that does get annoying after a while:

> "But didn't you promise—" Jessie said.
> "I did nothing of the sort," Tyrone said.
> "Now, look, you two . . ." Dudley said.
> "You stay out of this," Tyrone said.

If you substitute the occasional speaker attribution with a beat, you can break the monotony of the "saids" before it begins to call attention to itself.

> "But didn't you promise—" Jessie said.
> "I did nothing of the sort," Tyrone said.

Dudley stepped between them and held up his hands.

"Now look, you two . . ."

Tyrone spun on him. "You stay out of this."

Don't get carried away with the technique—it's best to replace only a few of your speaker attributions with beats. A beat after every line of dialogue is even more distracting than too many speaker attributions. What you want is a comfortable balance.

One or two final mechanical points. First, use dashes rather than ellipses, as in the example above, to show an interruption. Ellipses are used, in fiction at least, to show a character trailing off (as in the next to last line quoted above) or to show that there are gaps in the dialogue (as when you're showing one side of a telephone conversation).

And start a new paragraph whenever you have a new speaker. It will help your readers keep track of who's saying what. It's often a good idea to start a new paragraph for dialogue that follows a beat or bit of description, as in the "Dudley stepped between them . . ." in the example above. We'll return to frequent paragraphing later, but for now just keep in mind that good dialogue looks even better when you set it apart with its own paragraph.

CHECKLIST

• First, check your dialogue for explanations. It may help to take a highlighter and mark every place where an emotion is mentioned outside of dialogue. Chances are, most of them are explanations of one sort or another.

• Cut the explanations and see how the dialogue reads without them. Better? Worse? If it is worse, then start rewriting your dialogue.

• As long as you have your highlighter out, mark every -ly adverb. How many of them do you have? How many of them are based on adjectives describing an emotion (hysterically, angrily, morosely, and so forth)? You can probably do without most of them (though certainly not all).

• How about your speaker attributions? Any physical impossibilities ("he grimaced," "she snarled")? Any verbs other than "said"? Remember, though there are occasional exceptions, even innocuous verbs like "replied" or "answered" can call attention to themselves, especially if you don't use them very often.

• Can you get rid of some of your speaker attributions entirely? Just drop them and see if it's still clear who is speaking. Or try replacing some of them with beats.

• Have you started a paragraph with the speaker attribution?

• Pronoun before the noun (he said) rather than the other way around (said she)?

• Have you referred to a character more than one way in the same scene?

• Ellipsis for gaps, dashes for interruptions, right?

• How often have you paragraphed your dialogue? Try paragraphing a little more often and see how it reads.

EXERCISES
Try editing the following exchanges.

A. "You aren't seriously thinking about putting that trash in your body, are you?" said a voice from behind me, archly.

I put down the package of Twinkies and turned around. It was Fred McDermot, a passing acquaintance from work. "Pardon me?" I said.

"I said, you aren't going to put that stuff in your body, are you?" he repeated.

"Fred, I fail to see how that is any of your business," I chuckled.

"Paul, I'm just interested in your welfare, that's all," he replied. "Do you know what they put in those things?"

"No, Fred."

"Neither do I, Paul. That's the point."

B. Gatsby *redux. This novel was Fitzgerald's masterpiece and deserves its status as a modern classic. But literary fashions have changed since* Gatsby *was published, and techniques that were perfectly fine then seem cumbersome today. So this is your chance to edit a master. Don't look back at chapter one, and have fun.*

"I like to come," Lucille said. "I never care what I do, so I always have a good time. When I was here last, I tore my gown on a chair, and he asked me my name and address—within a week I got a package from Croirer's with a new evening gown in it."

"Did you keep it?" asked Jordan.

"Sure I did. I was going to wear it tonight, but it was too big in the bust and had to be altered. It was gas blue with lavender beads. Two hundred and sixty-five dollars."

"There's something funny about a fellow that'll do a thing like

that," said the other girl eagerly. "He doesn't want any trouble
with *any*body."

"Who doesn't?" I inquired.

"Gatsby. Somebody told me—"

The two girls and Jordan leaned together confidentially.

"Somebody told me they thought he killed a man."

A thrill passed over all of us. The three Mr. Mumbles bent forward and listened eagerly.

"I don't think it's so much *that*," argued Lucille skeptically;
"it's more that he was a German spy during the war."

One of the men nodded in confirmation.

"I heard that from a man who knew all about him, grew up
with him in Germany," he assured us positively.

"Oh, no," said the first girl, "it couldn't be that, because he
was in the American army during the war." As our credulity
switched back to her, she leaned forward with enthusiasm. "You
look at him sometimes when he thinks nobody's looking at him.
I'll bet he killed a man."

CHAPTER 5

....

SEE HOW IT SOUNDS

. . . the dialogue in the opening chapters is so exceptionally wretched ("How did you know it was me?" she said. "I have a mask on." "I only had to look for the most ostentatiously dressed woman, Scarlett. It was bound to be you."), so repetitive and inane, that one is driven to hoping it is the handiwork of one of the "book doctors" brought in to work on the poor corpse.

—MOLLY IVINS, reviewing *Scarlett, New York Times,*
October 27, 1991

As Ms. Ivins's review suggests (we'll overlook her dig at book doctors), the problem with dialogue is, more often than not, with the dialogue itself rather than with the mechanics. The creation of character voice—writing dialogue that lets your characters sound like who they really are—is one of the most creative and challenging acts you can commit as an author. Professional mechanics can make good dialogue dazzling, but what do you do if your dialogue is weak to begin with?

Contrary to popular wisdom, you can be taught to write better dialogue—a subject that would take a book of its own. In the meantime there are some mechanical techniques you can use when self-editing that will cure one of the most common reasons for flat voiceless dialogue: formality.

Of course, all dialogue is formal to some extent. If dialogue were an exact representation of the way most people actually talk most of the time, it would read like this:

"Good morning," he said.

"Good morning," she said.

"How was the weekend?"

"Oh, fine, fine. Got some stuff done."

"Oh yeah?"

"Yeah, yeah. Cut the lawn, trimmed the hedges, you know, things like that."

"Umm-humm."

"How about yourself?"

"Me? Uh, pretty much the same, I guess. Cut back the lilacs."

"Yeah, the lilacs. Grow like weeds, don't they?"

"Yeah."

If you were to write dialogue like this at novel length, your readers would nod off before they finished your first chapter. The dialogue you're trying to create has to be much more compressed, much more focused than real speech. In effect, dialogue is something artificial that sounds like real speech when you read it.

But most authors go overboard, creating dialogue so artificial that it becomes stilted and formal—again, it doesn't sound like anything anyone in their right mind, on this planet, in this century, would actually say. As a result, all the characters sound alike. Stilted speech is stilted speech no matter who speaks it.

The simplest way to make your dialogue less formal is to use more contractions. "I would not do that if I were you" sounds made up, where "I wouldn't do that if I were you" sounds like

"Contrary to popular wisdom
one can be taught to write better dialogue."

something a person would actually say. *You* use contractions,
and so should your characters. And if you want to convey that a
character is stiff—that he's pompous, or his first language isn't
English, or she's prissy—then dispensing with the contractions
is an elegant way to go. "Is it not wonderful" just has that Conti-
nental flair.

Another helpful technique is to use sentence fragments. Consider this exchange:

> "Is she pregnant?"
> "It doesn't matter whether she is or not. She's not going to marry him."

It sounds much less formal—and much more like real speech—if you edit it to read:

> "Is she pregnant?"
> "Doesn't matter whether she is or not, she's not going to marry him."

In the second exchange, the writer has used another technique (in addition to the sentence fragment) to good effect: the two sentences in the answer to the question are strung together with a comma instead of the (grammatically correct) period. If not overused, this technique captures remarkably well the rhythms of real speech.

If your dialogue seems formal, check also to make sure you aren't trying to shoehorn information into your dialogue that doesn't belong there. We've already suggested in Chapter 2 that you be wary of disguising your exposition as dialogue lest it make your characters speak out of character. It also tends to make dialogue stilted, as in:

> "Dear," she said, "I realize it seems unfair of me to tell you this now after eleven years of marriage and three children, but I'm afraid I'm not the woman I've led you to believe."

Again, you don't want your characters to speak more fully-formed thoughts than they normally would, just so you can get some information to your readers. This doesn't mean you should never use dialogue for exposition, of course—dialogue can be an excellent means of putting facts across to your read-

ers. Just make sure that your characters have a reason for saying the lines that you give them, and that the lines themselves
are in character.

Another way to make your dialogue more natural is to weed
out fancy polysyllabic words unless the use of them is right for
the character. "Have you considered the consequences?"
sounds like something you read in a book. "Have you thought
about what might happen?" sounds like something somebody
might actually say. So have your characters "think" rather than
"conclude"; "give up" rather than "surrender"; and "get" rather
than "retrieve." What you're going for is short words packed
full of consonants rather than longer, vowel-heavy words.

Another technique to loosen up your dialogue—one well
known to successful screenwriters—is misdirection. In formal
dialogue, questions are always clearly understood and answers
are complete and responsive. Real life is rarely that neat. Consider the difference between:

> "I don't know what you were thinking about, going into a
> place like that. Are you all right?"
> "I'm fine, really I am."

and

> "What did you think you were doing, going into a place like
> that?"
> "I'm all right. Really."

The first version is clear enough, but the bit of misdirection
in the second version gives the dialogue a little extra twist.

So have your characters misunderstand one another once in
a while. Have them answer the unspoken question rather than
the one asked out loud. Have them talk at cross-purposes.
Have them hedge. Disagree. Lie. It will go a long way toward
making them sound human.

For a striking example, notice the way Armand studiously

ignores the questions Richie asks in this passage from Elmore Leonard's *Killshot*:

> "Armand," Richie said, "you're not married, are you?"
> "No way."
> "You ever live with a woman? I mean outside your family?"
> "What's the point?"
> "Armand, lemme tell you something. You're always telling me something, now it's my turn. Okay, Armand." If he kept saying the name it would get easier. "You might have shot a woman or two in your line of work . . . . Have you?"
> "Go on what you're gonna tell me."
> "Let's say you have. But shooting a woman and understanding a woman are two entirely different things, man."

Had Armand simply answered Richie's questions or told Richie to shut up, the dialogue wouldn't have the subtle tension (and sense of authenticity) it does.

Take a look at the following passage of dialogue, from a workshop submission:

> "I wasn't expecting you until tomorrow," Anne said.
> "I thought it would be a nice idea to drop in."
> "Stan, I just got in about five minutes ago. I'm fixing myself something to eat and then I'm going to get some rest."
> "So what you're trying to tell me is that I'm not wanted. Right?"
> "Yes."

If you simply read it silently, this little snatch of dialogue probably seems fine. The mechanics are transparent, and Anne's exasperation with Stan is clear without being explained through speaker attributions. But try reading the example aloud. We did, and this is the result:

> "I wasn't expecting you until tomorrow," Anne said.
> "I just thought it would be nice to drop in, that's all."

"Stan, I just got in five minutes ago myself. All I want to do is fix something to eat and get some rest."

"Are you trying to tell me I'm not wanted?"

"You got it."

The changes we made were subtle, but if you read both examples aloud, you can see the difference they make. The second example reads more like real speech.

Again, good dialogue isn't an exact transcription of the way people talk but is more of an artifact, a literary device that mimics real speech. This means that dialogue is by nature slightly formal. And because most of the dialogue we read has this touch of formality, our eyes are trained to see slightly formal speech as normal. So if your dialogue is stiff or unnatural, you may not be able to spot the stiffness as you reread—your eye may pass right over it.

The answer of course is to bring your ear into play when you're editing yourself. After all, we're used to hearing relaxed, normal speech in real life. Much of the stiffness in a passage of dialogue that doesn't show up when you read your work silently (such as the "Yes" in the example above) will spring right out at you when you read out loud. You may find yourself making subtle little changes as you read. If so, pay attention to these changes—your ear is telling you how your dialogue should sound. The eye can be fooled but the ear knows.

In addition to helping you overcome stiffness, reading a passage aloud can help you find the rhythm of your dialogue. When and where to place your stage directions, when to insert a beat, when to let the dialogue push ahead—all of this becomes clearer when you hear your dialogue being spoken.

Some authors find it helpful to have a friend read through their dialogue with them, as if it were a screenplay. Others read their dialogue into a tape recorder and then play it back—the stiffness shows up more when they listen than when they read. But however you decide to do it, reading your dialogue aloud will almost always lead you to changes that make it sound more natural.

Reading dialogue aloud can help you distinguish between one character and another's way of speaking, too. Select a scene in which two or three characters speak, then go through it three times—reading aloud in turn all the lines spoken by a single character. As you read the first character's lines aloud, you may get a sense of his or her particular speech rhythms, vocabulary, conversational style (self-interruptive or self-contained, enthusiastic or rigid), speech mannerisms, and so forth. Then read the next character's lines aloud, and if the speech style is the same you know you've got some rethinking to do. As always when reading aloud, be alert for any "mistake" or change you make in the process of reading what's on the page or screen.

Everything we've just said about dialogue applies to narration and description as well. Consider the following:

> It had been Carl's rather desperate willingness to put himself and his home on display for the membership committee that finally convinced me that something concrete would have to be done about the longtime erosion of our marriage. The thought of joining such a group had never occurred to me, and I realized that Carl and I not only no longer thought the same way about things, we didn't even think about the same things.

Once again, the passage looks perfectly fine, but if you read it aloud, you will probably find yourself tripping over the wording from time to time—the "Carl and I not only no longer thought," for instance. As edited, the passage reads:

> Actually, it had been Carl's eagerness to put himself and his home (and his wife) on display for the membership committee that finally convinced me something specific would have to be done about the longtime erosion of our marriage. The thought of joining such a group had never occurred to me. I realized then that, not only did Carl and I no longer think the same way about things, we didn't even think about the same things.

Even writing that was never intended to be (and probably never will be) read aloud can be improved if you read aloud as you revise. Passages of narration and description will read better once they have the sense of rhythm and flow you edit in while (or after) reading them aloud.

A century ago, Mark Twain could write a novel full of passages like this one—

> "Why, Huck, doan' de French people talk de same way we does?"
>
> "*No*, Jim; you couldn't understand a word they said—not a single word."
>
> "Well, now, I be ding-busted! How do dat come?"
>
> "*I* don't know; but it's so. I got some of their jabber out of a book. Spose a man was to come to you and say *Polly-voo-franzy*—what would you think?"
>
> "I wouldn' think nuff'n; I'd take en bust him over de head."

—and get away with it.

Times have changed, and few authors today would write dialogue as hard to follow as Twain's. But beginning novelists even today are often tempted to write dialect—whether it be southern black or Bronx Italian or Locust Valley lockjaw—using a lot of trick spellings and lexical gimmicks. It's the easy way out.

And like most easy ways, it's not the best way. When you use an unusual spelling, you are bound to draw the reader's attention away from the dialogue and onto the means of getting it across. If the dialect gets thick enough, it isn't read so much as translated—as any twentieth-century reader of *Huckleberry Finn* could tell you. The occasional dropped *g* or common phonetic spelling such as "gonna" or "lemme" won't get you into trouble with your readers, but it doesn't take much to make too much.

If you think about it, there's a sense of nineteenth-century class consciousness to trick spellings. They hark back to a day when proper people spoke proper English properly. And if you had a character who was less than proper, like Jim in the quote above, you signaled his lack of proper background or education by spelling his dialogue the way he might spell it. Now that we know there is honor and dignity (or at least the potential for them) in anyone, whatever the education or income level, the trick spellings can go. So how *do* you get a character's geographical or educational or social background across? The best way is through word choice, cadence, and grammar. If you can capture the particular rhythm, the music in, say, a New England Yankee's way of speaking, you'll have put your character across without condescension and far more effectively.

Consider this example, taken from Ed McBain's review of *The Secret Pilgrim* by John le Carré:

> It comes as no surprise that le Carré's tone-perfect ear can recreate in English even the cadences and styles of people speaking in foreign tongues. Listen, for example, to the German girl Britta, a prisoner of the Israelis, talking to Ned in her native tongue, transcribed as English:
>
> "Are you inadequate, Mr. Nobody? I think perhaps you are. In your occupation, that is normal. You should join us, Mr. Nobody. You should take lessons with us, and we shall convert you to our cause. Then you will be adequate."
>
> Isn't that German we're reading?

And then there is the following example, from one of our authors:

> "I didn't stay up to fight," she said. "But I got to find out what it is keeping us here. What it is keeping my children from being somebody."
>
> "They already be somebody. They *born* somebodies."
>
> "Somebody to do what? Work the cane field? All I want is what's good for us and the children."
>
> "You making me crazy, that's what you doing. I used to could

forget about the cane field at night. I used to not remember about my papa and mama so much. Now—"

"If we left here, you wouldn't seen the cane field no more. You wouldn't have nightmares about your papa and your mama, neither. I can't understand why you stay."

"Why I got to give you a reason? Reason ain't no pain killer. Reason ain't no free-feeling good world."

Notice that the author never changes a spelling, never even drops a *g*. There are no explanations, no adverbs, and no speaker attributions beyond the first one. There is one interruption, one bit of misdirection, and neither of the characters speaks more than three sentences in a row.

But read the passage aloud. When you do, you can feel how right the words are, how well they fit the mouths of the author's southern black characters. It takes courage to write a line like "Reason ain't no free-feeling good world." But the results are worth the risk. You can imagine real, live people saying these words.

That's what you should strive for in all of your dialogue—to give a sense that the words you write are words real people would actually speak. Explanations, adverbs, oddball verbs of speech, trick spellings—these can't really help your dialogue because they don't really change the dialogue. They take the place of good dialogue rather than helping create it.

And if you're serious about writing fiction well, you will accept no substitutes.

CHECKLIST

• First, read your dialogue aloud. Read your narration out loud, for that matter. At some point or another, you should read aloud every word you write.

• As you read, be on the lookout for places where you are tempted to change the wording. Give in to this temptation whenever you can.

• How smooth and polished is your dialogue? Could you use more contractions, more sentence fragments, more run-on sentences?

• Is your stiff dialogue really exposition in disguise?

• How well do your characters understand one another? Do they ever mislead one another? Any outright lies?

• How about dialect? Are you using a lot of unusual spellings and other lexical tricks? If you rewrite your dialect with standard spellings, does it still read like dialect?

EXERCISES

A. This exercise was taken from one of our workshop submissions. Try to edit it so as to get rid of some of the formality.

As they sat quietly catching their breath, Getz said, "We've all been diving together for a long time and are very comfortable with each other. I understand you're experienced but you are new to us, so I wonder if you would mind my giving you a quick quiz, just to satisfy ourselves of your basic competence?"

"Go ahead, sir."

"Okay, this is easy. What is your maximum no-decompress bottom time at three atmospheres?"

"The U.S. Navy tables allow sixty minutes at sixty feet with a standard rate of ascent."

"Good work, Mr. Wheeler. Welcome aboard. You see, we try not to take chances. We are frequently more than ten hours from a competent physician and there is no recompression chamber in the country. We don't 'push the tables.'"

Lou grinned boyishly, speaking with a cigarette in his mouth.

"You mean we don't *regularly* 'push the tables.'"

B. *The following passage was originally written by one of the authors of this book as a workshop exercise. Be forewarned, it includes every dialogue point we've made in the last two chapters, and a few points we will make in chapters yet to come.*

I peered through the front window of the garage, which did me no good since light hadn't been able to penetrate that window since man landed on the moon. "Anybody here?" I tapped on the door.

A man came out from the shop wearing greasy, half-unzipped coveralls with the name "Lester" stitched in over the pocket. I hoped he took those off before he got into my car.

"Yeah, wha' can I do for youse?" he grumbled as he took his cigar stub out of his mouth and spat near my feet.

"Well, my name is Mr. Baumgarten. I'm here to pick up my car. Is it ready?" I said sweetly. Truth is, I was ready to get the car away from him whether it was ready or not.

"Hang onna sec.' He stepped back into the shop and picked up a greasy clipboard with a thick wad of forms under the clip. "Wha' wuzza name again, Bumgarden?"

"BAUMgarten." I said. You cretin, I thought.

"Yeah, right," he said, pawing through the forms. "Don' see youse here, Mr. BAUMgarden. Sorry."

"What do you mean, sorry? You have my car in there. Either it's fixed or it's not." I'm a patient man, but my blood was beginning to boil.

"Loo, mistah, whaddya think—I got time to get, like, intimit wid all my clientele?" Oh, I bet you get intimate if they're pretty enough, I thought. "You could be BAUMgarden, you could be his cousin, you could be Governor Cuomo for all I know," he went on. "But I ain't givin you no car 'less you got papers and I got matchin' papers. Far as I'm concerned, you ain't on this clipboard, you don't exist."

....

CHAPTER 6

INTERIOR MONOLOGUE

Big Jim Billups fondled the .38 in his pocket, waddled over to the back of his truck, and spat. Could've stopped the whole damn thing last night—they don't carry no guns. What was the use of doing a job if you didn't do a good one? He rocked, shifting his weight from one leg to another and spat again. The sound of the marchers was closer now.

Soon it would be time.

Yes, fiction has become more like movies and television over the past few decades as authors rely on immediate scenes from specific points of view to put their stories across. And, yes, you can convey a great many things on film that can't be conveyed on the page. But fiction has a reliable, powerful advantage over film: it's much easier to place a reader than a moviegoer in someone else's head. If the example quoted above were to be filmed, a skillful actor (Nick Nolte, say) could show that Big Jim is waiting for something, that he's nervous, and that he's a bit disgusted. The viewers would never know what he was waiting for or why he felt the way he did.

But on the page, readers move easily from the description of Big Jim's actions to Big Jim's thoughts and back again without ever being aware that anything out of the ordinary is happening. And yet what's happening is, when you think about it, remarkable. We're being allowed to see the world, if only for a moment, through someone else's eyes. One of the great gifts of literature is that it allows for the expression of unexpressed thoughts: in other words, interior monologue.

Interior monologue allows you not only to disclose information that would be hard to bring out in dialogue (such as who and what Big Jim is waiting for) but also to give your readers a feel for who your characters are. There is, arguably, no easier way to explore a character or express a reaction to events than through interior monologue. After all, you can let your readers in on exactly what your characters really think without having to filter that thought through dialogue and action. Interior monologue is an intimate, powerful way to establish a character's voice—and personality.

And, as you might expect, interior monologue is so powerful and easy to write (though not easy to write well) that many fiction writers tend to overuse it. Take a look at the passage that follows:

> "Mike, why are you here?" She asked this in what she hoped sounded like a neutral and reasonable tone. She knew how close she was to losing her defenses and made a special effort to pull back and regard Mike with professional distance.
>
> "I need your help," he said.
>
> "Why come to me?" After all, he knew she hated him.
>
> "Because I trust you."
>
> Laura shook her head and pulled a note pad from the top drawer of her desk.
>
> "I'll give you the names of three excellent therapists," she said, head buried in the paper, "and you can choose the one you feel most comfortable with."

"Not that kind of help." His voice was commanding and demanding simultaneously. "No, this is in the nature of police work."

Laura felt herself becoming angry at him and his intrusion into her life. The sooner he left the better.

"Get to the point, Mike."

If you're like most readers, you found this passage a little irritating. Constant interruptions are just as annoying on the page as they are in life, and this author has interrupted her dialogue with interior monologue over and over again. Just about every line is followed by an excursion into Laura's head.

Some of these monologues express thoughts that are already clear from the dialogue itself ("He knew she hated him"). And many of them are actually dialogue explanations in disguise ("Laura felt herself becoming angry . . ."). But even if all of them were legitimate, insightful passages of interior monologue, there are just too many of them for reading comfort. The interior monologue, instead of adding to the characterization and the flow of the scene, gets in the way. Take a look at the scene again with the interior monologue edited out:

"Mike, why are you here?" She hoped this sounded neutral, reasonable. It was everything she could do to keep her defenses in place.

"I need your help," he said.

"Why come to me?"

"Because I trust you."

Laura shook her head and pulled a note pad from the top drawer of her desk.

"I'll give you the names of three excellent therapists," she said, "and you can choose the one you feel most comfortable with."

"Not that kind of help. This is more in the nature of police work."

She slammed the notebook down on her desk. "Get to the point."

Note that we've left only enough interior monologue to give the readers an idea as to what's going on in Laura's head—all the explanations and dialogue descriptions are gone. Interior monologue is best served up a little at a time, especially in a dialogue scene, as a support for dialogue rather than a substitute for it.

Assuming you trim out all your unneeded interior monologue, how do you handle what's left so that it reads smoothly and professionally? The sterling virtue of interior monologue mechanics, once again, is unobtrusiveness. First: Never, ever, use quotes with your interior monologue. It is not merely poor style; it is, by today's standards, ungrammatical. Thoughts are thought, not spoken. Also, don't have your characters mumble to themselves or speak softly under their breath:

> "Yes, sir, I'll get right on it sir," he said, then muttered, "Soon as I finish lunch."

As a way of getting interior monologue across, the technique is contrived and usually unnecessary.

And if you want your interior monologue to be unobtrusive to the point of transparency, get rid of what are, in effect, speaker attributions.

> Had he meant to kill her? Not likely, he thought.

> Had he meant to kill her? Not likely.

Remember, the purpose of speaker attributions is to let your readers know who is speaking when. Since each scene you write will be from a single point of view (and it will, won't it?), you usually won't need to attribute your interior monologue. Your readers will know immediately who the thoughts belong to. In fact, you can tell this method is working if you can still tell that the thought is a thought—and, in context, *whose* thought—without the speaker attribution.

If you're writing in the third person, you can just write your

"So far all her dreams have not come true but she wants high romance and a baby while her husband wants to be, and is, a very successful broker, who takes graduate courses at night and wants no baby and at the same time she has more or less recovered from being in love with the well-digger who dug her well, which is good since he is married with three children and is a drug addict and an alcoholic and he claims he's dying, although there are no signs of this and she says once she finds an outlet for her unrequited love she will lose eighty-five pounds. I enjoyed that sentence."

interior monologue in third rather than first person:

I always end up killing them, he thought.

He always ended up killing them.

You can easily get rid of the "he wondered" locution by converting a short passage of interior monologue into a question (we call it the Q trick):

> He wondered why he always ended up killing them.
>
> Why did he always end up killing them?

Longer passages of interior monologue can sometimes be set off in their own paragraph:

> Monroe settled into one of the plastic chairs outside the examining room and flipped through a magazine.
> Who was he kidding, he knew he couldn't read anything in the state he was in. Still, better to look at the pictures in the ads than to stare at the other patients. Or worse yet, to think about what was about to happen.

If you apply these techniques faithfully, and if your viewpoint character has a strong, distinctive voice, you will eventually see the line between interior monologue and description blur slightly. After all, your readers will know they're seeing the world through your character's eyes (from the narrative voice), and it's not a big jump from a character's eyes to a character's mind. Consider the following passage, from one of our workshop submissions:

> He flipped the book over and stared at the quote. "A masterpiece of clarity and insight by a leading clinician and theoretician." The words were from Jerome Carver, Jr., M.D.
> Pond hurled the book at the wall.
> Jerry Carver was Pond's best friend, the one who'd run off with Alice after Pond was released from prison. Just when he'd needed them most. The attribution should have read Jerome Carver, Jr., TRAITOR.

The first two paragraphs of this passage are clearly description, but with the third, the distinction becomes a bit less obvious. The paragraph starts out with what looks like backstory, yet by the time the paragraph is finished, it's clear we're being let into Pond's mind. The transition is so smooth the seams don't show.

And then there is this celebrated passage from James Joyce's *Portrait of the Artist as a Young Man*:

A girl stood before him in midstream, alone and still, gazing out to sea. She seemed like one whom magic had changed into the likeness of a strange and beautiful seabird. Her long slender bare legs were delicate as a crane's and pure save where an emerald trail of seaweed had fashioned itself as a sign upon the flesh. Her thighs, fuller and softhued as ivory, were bared almost to the hips where the white fringes of her drawers were like feathering of soft white down. Her slateblue skirts were kilted boldly about her waist and dovetailed behind her. Her bosom was as a bird's, soft and slight, slight and soft as the breast of some darkplumaged dove. But her long fair hair was girlish: and girlish, and touched with the wonder of mortal beauty, her face.

She was alone and still, gazing out to sea; and when she felt his presence and the worship of his eyes her eyes turned to him in quiet sufferance of his gaze, without shame or wantonness. Long, long she suffered his gaze and then quietly withdrew her eyes from his and bent them towards the stream, gently stirring the water with her foot hither and thither. The first faint noise of gently moving water broke the silence, low and faint and whispering, faint as the bells of sleep; hither and thither, hither and thither: and a faint flame trembled on her cheek.

—Heavenly God! cried Stephen's soul, in an outburst of profane joy.

He turned away from her suddenly and set off across the strand. His cheeks were aflame; his body was aglow; his limbs were trembling. On and on and on and on he strode, far out over the sands, singing wildly to the sea, crying to greet the advent of the life that had cried to him.

In this passage Stephen Dedalus turns away from the seashore changed forever. What's extraordinary is that in the context of the novel as a whole we know why he is changed forever, because *we experience the change with him*. Joyce draws us into Stephen Dedalus's head in a way no writer before him had done. In the process, he provided a reading experience Sean O'Faolin described in 1955 as "so mesmeric, so hypnotic . . . that I can never speak of it to young readers without murmuring, *Enter these enchanted woods ye who dare*."

The techniques we've been talking about are most effective when your narrative voice is also your character's voice—when you are writing not only through your character's eyes but also through his or her mind. As we said in the last chapter, there are going to be times when you don't want this intimate contact, when you want to put a little distance between your readers and your viewpoint character. (Three hundred pages of the kind of intensity Joyce creates in the above passage would be exhausting.) When you write in a more neutral, authorial voice, the distinction between description and interior monologue becomes sharper.

You can still make the shift from straightforward description to interior monologue by giving the monologue its own paragraph. As in the following example from Garrison Keillor's *WLT: A Radio Romance*:

> Delores could be a Mafia gun moll who calls Chicago late at night and conducts mysterious business with a man named Gino, talking tough talk with a cigarette dangling from her lips . . . Frank offers to help with her suitcase and it falls open and bundles of fresh C-notes tumble out and she says, "Freeze, buster, I got two guns concealed in my blouse and they're both pointed at you now!"
>
> Well, maybe not her blouse.

You can also use italics to set off interior monologue, as in this passage from an unpublished novel by Judith Searle, one of our editors:

> And she was now six weeks without work. Amazing what that had done to her self-confidence. There were moments when she

actually wondered if she had lost it, that magical ability to—*stop it! The last thing you need is to get depressed.*

Two caveats about italics (and, in fact, about unusual typefaces in general). Since long passages in italics are a pain to read, you can only use this technique effectively for passages no longer than a sentence or two. Even this brief passage is too long, don't you think? Also, since generations of hacks have used italics to punch up otherwise weak dialogue ("I have just about *had* it up to *here* with your get-rich-quick schemes!"), frequent italics have come to signal weak writing. So you should *never* resort to them unless they are the *only* practical choice. In the passage above, the author was working on two different levels of interior monologue, with one interrupting the other. She *needed* the italics to *distinguish* between the two. But unless you really *need* italics they're just plain *irritating*, aren't they?

Italics are a particularly good way to signal interior monologue when it's desirable for some reason to disclose a character's thought in the middle of an action scene:

He had just pulled the mail out of the box and was unlocking the door when he heard the creak. He glanced back in time to see the old Chevy's front wheel ride over the brick he'd chocked it with. Then the whole car began to roll ponderously down the driveway.

He broke into a sprint. The car was moving more quickly than it seemed to be, but he managed to catch up to it and grab hold of the back bumper.

Great, now what?

He stopped, panting, and simply stood and watched as the car sailed off the retaining wall at the driveway's bottom.

The italicized sentence is brief enough that it doesn't interrupt the action, yet it adds something that would be hard to work into the scene without interior monologue. Also the contrast between the objective picture of what's going on and the glimpse into the main character's head acts almost like a cinematic jump cut to turn up the tension of the scene.

One final caveat. When you're self-editing, be on the lookout for long passages of interior monologue. As we've suggested, they usually mean you are telling the reader things you should be showing. If you have Inspector Bowman sit at a quiet table in the pub and go over the facts of the case in his mind, you are dangerously close to narrating the facts of the case for your readers. Far better to give Bowman a sidekick to talk things over with. In general, consider the possibility that any passage of interior monologue more than a page long may need cutting, breaking up, or conversion to a scene.

There are many exceptions, of course. You might want to use a fairly lengthy running commentary to introduce your readers to several characters at once, or to describe a particular setting as one of your characters would see it. (Think of the way Rex Stout's Archie Goodwin used to size up everyone who entered Nero Wolfe's office.)

And there may also be times when you want to show your characters in some unusual state of mind—descending into madness or drunkenness, or having an epiphany, or even a dream. Keeping your readers in the claustrophobic mind of a paranoid, for instance, could be a terrific way to turn up the tension at a key point in your plot.

Take a look at this example from an excellent first novel we worked on recently:

[Dr. Morris Fitzmaurice is a chemical researcher who, for reasons we can't get into now, has been sinking slowly into drug-crazed delirium. He is about to meet with the board of directors to discuss his funding.]

He entered the board room and discovered a reeling, chaotic mess. All of the walls billowed with a hot demonic wind. The twelve members of the board had taken on bestial aspects (or perhaps he was seeing them for the first time as they truly were), and Morris instantly perceived that the roast beef sandwiches they devoured as they waited for him in many ways symbolized their way of life—carnivorous, preying on the flesh of those weaker and slower. Jolas looked up at him with blood staining his teeth and smiled a smile that was more than fifty percent leer and Tinsdale reached out to take his hand as if to give one's hand in some way meant to acquiesce, to agree with the corrupt morals of these animals, to shake and in a sense wash one's hands of the slow rape of the environment which their kind endorsed, as they had since first a king declared himself to be better than those around him and raised around himself a noble class to aid him in living well off the sweat of others' brows just as these men had taken Morris's ideas and labor and bought themselves houses in Greenwich and Westport with tennis courts and pools, where their Negro servants came in to do their manual labor for them and they probably porked the maid while their wives were away and then when she had their illegitimate kid paid her to go live in Florida because she wasn't educated and didn't know she could get child support and she went along just like his grandfather had when these bastards came in and drove him off his farm his whole life and pushed him to drink and eventually killed him far younger than he should have died and now they sat smugly in their upholstered chairs and because they had money and power they expected Morris to suck the slime out from between their sweaty toes. Well, he wouldn't do it!

With his empty bottle of Cuervo Gold held aloft, the first words Morris spoke to the Board of Directors of Exeter Chemical were these:

"You filthy negro-maid-fuckers, you killed my grandfather. You bastards are going to burn in hell for the next thousand years. Your next twenty-three incarnations will be as cockroaches. Die, verminous scum."

That's the gist of how Dr. Morris Fitzmaurice lost his job at Exeter Chemical.

Notice that the last three paragraphs are written from the omniscient point of view—which is fortunate, since a page or two inside Morris's head is all most readers could stand. In fact, the author has used point of view skillfully throughout the book. Most of the first part of the story is written firmly from Morris's point of view, but as Morris gets crazier and crazier, the narrative viewpoint becomes more and more detached. By this point in the novel, the author is writing primarily in the omniscient point of view, except for occasional paragraphs such as the above where he lets us in on what's going on in Morris' chemical-ravaged brain.

Or take a look at this example, from a novel-in-progress by Fran Dorf:

[Lee Green, a white, well-to-do author, has been struggling to write from the point of view of a black prisoner.]

She stared at what she had written, read it and reread it. Then she began working with it, cautiously at first, taking single words on the screen and replacing them with other words, or adding an adjective here and there and removing it. Then she changed whole blocks of copy, added new sentences, removed others, changed others, molding the words on the screen like a piece of wet clay—

Wait a minute. What she had written wasn't right. The screw's name wasn't O'Connor. It was Dolgin, and he was short and pudgy with rotting gums. And the word was he was getting rich off the joint, selling the pimps drugs.

And the view from the cell was wrong too. Unless you stood on tiptoe or hunched way down, you couldn't even see the levels above and below you. You could see McGrath directly across from you ,and he would be reading, and to his left Booker would be crying, and to his left Scoggins, the fuck, would be sitting on the goddamned pot again. And to Scoggins' left you could see Arnie Wells, who sometimes played with himself as if no one could see. And sometimes, at night, after lights out, if you stood up and craned your neck you might catch a glimpse of McCracken, and he would be pacing his cell in the dark.

Notice that the mechanics of the interior monologue are completely transparent—no speaker attributions, no italics.

Yet it's perfectly clear that we are inside Lee's head as she suddenly finds herself inside the head of a real prisoner in a maximum security prison. This segue from one head to another, so difficult to show on film, is almost effortless in print.

That is the power of interior monologue.

CHECKLIST

•First, how much interior monologue do you have? You might want to take out the highlighter again and highlight every passage that occurs inside someone's head.

•If you seem to have a lot, check to see whether some of your interior monologue is actually dialogue descriptions in disguise. Are you using interior monologue to show things that should be told? Should some of your longer passages be turned into scenes?

•Do you use speaker attributions with your interior monologue (perhaps they should be called thinker attributions)? If you simply drop the attributions, is it still clear that your character's thoughts are thought rather than spoken?

•Can you get rid of your thinker attributions by converting the interior monologue from first to third person? By giving it its own paragraph? Converting it into a question? *Italicizing* it?

•How close are your narrative voice and your character's voice? In other words, how much distance is there between your characters and your readers? Is it as much distance as you intended? As your reader needs?

EXERCISES
Try your hand at the following:

A. "Excuse me, miss, but I'm giving a seminar over in

Room 206 in a few minutes, and I need an overhead projector." The man at the door of the audio-visual room was actually wearing a tweed jacket with leather patches at the elbows. *All he needs is a pipe,* Kimberly thought.

"Okay, if you want an overhead or something like that—a movie projector or slides or whatever—you have to fill out a form ahead of time," she said briskly. "Then we can, like, line everything up and—"

"I know. I sent in the form three weeks ago."

Okay, she thought, that would have been when Ed was still in charge of AV and he would have taken care of this, wouldn't he? I mean, Ed was a little sloppy—I'm going to have to clean up the office when I get a chance—but he basically got things done.

"You've been up to the seminar room?" she said.

"Yes," he replied, "and the projector wasn't there."

Oh God, she thought. Great, I've only been in charge for fifteen minutes and already there's a major screw up. "Okay, do your have your, whadya call it, your course form?"

He snapped the briefcase open, reached into it, and

pulled out the familiar green card. "Right here."

Yeah, there it was, right on the form where it was supposed to be. "Give me a minute."

She ducked into the office and dug out the clipboard with all the requisitions on it. After five minutes, he got tired of waiting and stuck his head in the office.

"Miss? I don't want to be late," he said irritably.

"All right, mister." Jeez, she thought, he could at least give her a little time. "What's the course number."

"A3205."

She went through the forms again. *Definitely no A3205 there.* "What's the room number."

"As I believe I told you, it's 206. I don't suppose you could just give me a projector now, could you? I'd be happy to carry it over myself."

"Nope, we don't have any to spare. If you want one, we have to figure out where yours went." She ruffled through the forms one more time. Suddenly she found it. "Okay, here's the problem. I have Room 206 listed as

A9631, 'Making Fresh Baby Food at Home.' The projector should be up there."

"Miss, the projector's not there," he said drily. "That's why I'm here."

Jeez, she wondered what it would take to please this guy. "You're sure it's not there? Did you check the closet."

"Room 206 doesn't have a closet."

"It most certainly does. It's the big seminar room off the cafeteria, right?"

"No, it's a smallish room near the elevators. How long have you worked here?"

"Long enough to know the building." *So there,* she thought. "Did you come across the courtyard to get here?"

"Um, yes, I did."

Ha, she had him. "Okay, we don't handle that wing of the building. You want the AV room for the Peebles annex, it's down by the bursar's office."

"Oh, I see." He looked at his watch. "Well, thank you."

"Hey, no sweat. We're here to serve."

B. Norm looked at the finished doorframe for the patio doors. All he had to do now was hang the doors themselves, then after the electrician futzed around for a few more days, the living room would be ready for drywall. It was his favorite stage in a construction project—when the place he was building began to actually look like a house.

"Excuse me, Norm?"

"Yes, Mrs. Kincaid." The homeowner. *There is nothing I love more than to have the homeowner on site at this stage in the game.*

"I was wondering, will the doors actually be that narrow."

And this is why. What does she think, we're going to put in doors six inches wider than the frames?

"Yes ma'am, I'm afraid so," he said.

"Do you suppose we could make them a little bit wider? Not much, say a foot or so on each side?"

Ah, the joy of cost overruns. We'll just remove those two load-bearing members, which we can probably get away with if we reinforce the corner posts and run an I-beam between them. It will mean restructuring the entire front of the house,

but we can do it. And then we'll throw away those doors we

had custom made and have some new ones custom made.

"Well, it might cost a little extra."

"Oh, but I think it would be worth it. Just imagine the

extra light the wider doors would bring."

Just imagine the yacht I'm going to buy with the proceeds.

"All right, ma'am, I'll get right on it."

C. *Read through these five passages once for enjoyment, then
reread them and notice the way—or ways—the author has handled interior monologue (none of them uses speaker attribution):*

Now Frank had almost gotten his breath back after it was

knocked out of him. Still, there was nothing to say, except *Please*

come with me, please, and I will make it be wonderful, oh yes, I

will make your life happy forever and ever, and he couldn't say it.

"I think you would like Merle if you ever met him," she said.

"He's smart. He's very funny."

I hope his train crashes and falls into Lake Pepin.

"Oh. What's he up to these days?"

"He's trying out for a road show called *Yippee-Ay* that he'd like me to try out for, too. A big musical revue with dancers and trapeze acts and elephants, and he said they have a small speaking role that'd be perfect for me, the part of a Chinese girl, but I'd have to ride an elephant and be in this number where you hang by your ankle fifty feet in the air and a guy twirls you for awhile. But I guess I could do it."

Frank was nearly tearing an envelope into squares and arranging them in facing rows, like houses. Why was she telling him this? The less he heard about Merle, the better. On the other hand—maybe—she *had* to tell him because he was the only one who could talk her out of this Merle foolishness and get her to see what she already knew but couldn't bring herself to say, which was that she loved him. Loved Frank. *Listen*.
—Garrison Keillor, *WLT: A Radio Romance*

"Go on back in that house and get to bed."

"You have to touch me. On the inside part. And you have to call me my name." As long as his eyes were locked on the silver of the lard can he was safe. If he trembled like Lot's wife and felt some womanish need to see the nature of the sin behind him; feel a sympathy, perhaps, for the cursing cursed, or want to hold it in his arms out of respect for the connection between them, he

too would be lost.

—TONI MORRISON, *Beloved*

Vincent asked, "Does it help if I tell you I love you, or does it

make it worse?"

She began to cry. It was the second time in two days, but its

effect on Vincent was not dimmed by repetition.

"Okay," she said. "Here goes."

His heart seemed to stop. This was it, but what was it?

—LAURIE COLWIN, *Happy All the Time*

But Marie had stayed apart from everyone. She sat in the dust of

the clearing on the other side of the poles, watching over her father

from dawn till night. Even when they hauled her mother from the

stockade and her screams for Hansen rang out from behind the

hillock, changing to screams for mercy and ending with the usual

pistol shot, Marie's eyes never flinched from Hansen's face.

"Did she know?" I asked in French.

"The whole camp knew."

"Had she been fond of her mother?"

Was it my imagination or had Hansen closed his eyes in the darkness?

"I was the father of Marie," he replied. "I was not the father of their relationship."
—JOHN LE CARRÉ, *The Secret Pilgrim*

I looked up to see a young man with brown and luminous spaniel eyes, shaggy brown hair, an aggressively badly cut tweed jacket such as German intellectuals wear in Munchen or Berlin and a pleading mouth...

"Wolfgang Schnabel," he offered. "May I?"

"Of course," I said, sighing.

"But, I interrupt your thoughts?"

"No, no," I said. (What woman has thoughts that cannot be interrupted by a man?)
—ERICA JONG, *Serenissima*

Now enjoy the experience of editing five modern masters who write immensely effective interior monologue—that would be even more effective without the speaker attributions:

There ought to be a whole separate language, she thought, for words that are truer than other words—for perfect, absolute truth. It was the purest fact of her life: she did not understand him, and she never would.

—ANNE TYLER, *Dinner at the Homesick Restaurant*

"You see," Smiley explained, "our obsession with virtue won't go away. Self-interest is so *limiting*. So is expediency." He paused again, still deep inside his own thoughts. "All I'm really saying, I suppose, is that if the temptation to humanity does assail you now and then, I hope you won't take it as a weakness in yourselves, but give it a fair hearing." The cufflinks, I thought, in a flash of inspiration. George is remembering the old man.

—JOHN LE CARRÉ, *The Secret Pilgrim*

"Did you go up there? When you were young?"

"I went to dances," the doctor said. "I specialized in getting Cokes for people. I was extremely good at getting Cokes passed around." He helped her into a chair. "Now, then, what can I do for you?"

Amanda sat her pocketbook down on the floor and told him what she had come for.

Jesus Christ, he thought, wondering how many years he would

have to practice medicine before he learned never to be sur-

prised at anything.

—ELLEN GILCHRIST, *The Annunciation*

Dalgleish thought, This isn't my case and I can't stop him by

force. But at least he could ensure that the direct path to the

body lay undisturbed. Without another word he led the way and

Mair followed. Why this insistence, he wondered, on seeing the

body? To satisfy himself that she was in fact, dead, the scientist's

need to verify and confirm? Or was he trying to exorcise a horror

he knew could be more terrible in imagination than in reality?

Or was there, perhaps, a deeper compulsion, the need to pay her

the tribute of standing over her body in the quietness and loneli-

ness of the night before the police arrived with all the official

paraphernalia of a murder investigation to violate forever the

intimacies they had shared.

—P.D. JAMES, *A Taste for Death*

Of course, I thought, Owen has the ball. He was a collector;

one had to consider only his baseball cards. "After all," Mr. Chick-

ering would say—in later years—"it was the only decent hit the kid ever made, the only real wood he ever got on the ball. And

even then, it was a foul ball. Not to mention that it killed some-

one."

   So what if Owen has the ball? I was thinking.
   —JOHN IRVING, *A Prayer for Owen Meany*

EASY BEATS

"Laura's illness is very complex," I said. "If you'd just—"

"My wife obviously has a screw loose somewhere," he said. "I was under the impression that the family is informed when a person goes crazy."

I sighed. "Sometimes that's true," I admitted.

He said, "But you don't think my wife is crazy, or what?"

My frustration was mounting. "I wish you'd stop throwing that word around so casually," I snapped.

"I don't give a goddamn what you wish," he said. "It's obvious to me that my wife should be in an asylum."

What an odd choice of word, I thought. "There are no asylums any more, Mr. Wade," I pointed out.

He got up, walked over to the window and looked out, then turned back to me.

"Whatever," he said. "A hospital, then."

I took off my glasses, rubbed my eyes. "Why do you think she should be in a hospital?" I asked him.

"Delusions. You've heard of them?"

"Once or twice." I said sarcastically, beginning to lose it. "Why don't you tell me about Laura's?"

"Thinking things that are obviously ridiculous," he said. "Misinterpreting everyday events and people's behavior as having something to do with her—with this power she thinks she has. Oh, but I forgot. You believe in witches."

By now you will be able to spot several problems with the dialogue in this example, taken from an early draft of Fran Dorf's *A Reasonable Madness*. There are some explanatory speaker attributions (and one thinker attribution), several dialogue descriptions, and one *-ly* adverb. Yet if you read the example carefully, you can see that underneath these mechanical problems lies some dialogue with real snap to it. The dialogue explanations mask the tension of the scene, but that tension is still there.

As you can see if you read the passage with its unnecessary dialogue mechanics edited out:

"Laura's illness is very complex," I said. "If you'd just—"

"My wife obviously has a screw loose somewhere," he said. "I was under the impression that the family is informed when a person goes crazy."

I sighed. "Sometimes that's true."

"But you don't think my wife is crazy, or what?"

My frustration was mounting. "I wish you'd stop throwing that word around so casually."

"I don't give a goddamn what you wish. It's obvious to me that my wife should be in an asylum."

What an odd choice of word. "There are no asylums any more, Mr. Wade."

He got up, walked over to the window and looked out, then turned back to me.

"Whatever," he said. "A hospital, then."

I took off my glasses, rubbed my eyes. "Why do you think she should be in a hospital?" I asked him.

"Delusions. You've heard of them?"

"Why don't you tell me what you think those are, Mr. Wade?"

"Thinking things that are obviously ridiculous," he said. "Misinterpreting everyday events and people's behavior as having something to do with her—with this power she thinks she has. Oh, but I forgot. You believe in witches."

The tension is mounting, yes, but it still falls short of the relentlessness it *could* have. Now take a look at the passage as finally edited:

"Laura's illness is very complex. If you'd—"

"My wife obviously has a screw loose somewhere," he said. "I was under the impression that the family is informed when a person goes crazy."

"Well, yes," I said, "But—"

"But you don't think my wife is crazy, or what?"

"I wish you'd stop throwing that word around."

"I don't give a goddamn what you wish. It's obvious to me that my wife belongs in an asylum."

An asylum?

"There are no asylums any more, Mr. Wade."

"A hospital, then. Whatever."

I took off my glasses, rubbed my eyes. "Why do you think Laura belongs in a hospital?"

"Delusions. You've heard of them?"

"Why don't you tell me what you think those are, Mr. Wade."

"Thinking things that are obviously ridiculous," he said. "Misinterpreting everyday events and people's behavior as having something to do with her—with this power she thinks she has. Oh, but I forgot. You believe in witches."

Now the tension is on the surface—you can feel it crackling between the two men. What's the difference? Self-editing for dialogue points helped, but what really improves the flow of the scene is the fact that in the second version the dialogue is interrupted less often. The revision contains fewer beats.

Beats?

Beats are the little bits of action interspersed through a scene, such as a character walking to a window or removing his glasses and rubbing his eyes—the literary equivalent of what is known in the theater as stage business. Usually they involve physical gestures, although short passages of interior monologue can also be considered a sort of internal beat.

For instance, the following passage, from Barbara Kingsolver's *Animal Dreams*, has only one beat—and it's a good one:

> "You don't have to talk about this," I said.
> "I don't ever talk about him. Sometimes I'll go a day or two without even thinking about him, and then I get scared I might forget he ever was."
> I laid a hand on his gearshift arm. "You want me to drive?"

Beats enable your readers to picture the action in a scene, allow you to vary the rhythm of the dialogue, and help reveal your character's personalities. In effect, they remind your readers of who your characters are and what they are doing. In Kingsolver's scene, the beat—"I laid a hand on his gearshift arm"—makes the driver's sadness over his brother's death more real to us and at the same time conveys the narrator's compassion.

If good beats come easily to you, be careful not to get carried away with the use of them. You don't want to interrupt your dialogue so often—with beats or interior monologue—that the flow of the scene is damaged. In the last chapter, we suggested that you resist the temptation to use interior monologue to track your character's emotions, which turns the interior monologue into a running commentary on the dialogue. The same thing often happens with beats.

Consider this example from Jill Robinson's *Dr. Rocksinger and the Age of Longing*:

> Hedy picked up some apples I'd glazed from the first bushel I'd bought. "You and apples." He put them back in the old bird's nest I kept them in. "Let's put on some music."

©BOOTH

"Bear in mind as you use beats to vary the rhythm, like a piece of fine music, your dialogue should have an ebb and flow to it .... Get your feet out of my face! .... You Rat-nosed Git !! ....."

I thought it might wake the children. But I decided not to mention that. I did sometimes play music when I was working. He saw me hesitate.

"Are you worried about waking the kids? We don't have to."

"Oh, they're used to it." I didn't say it was almost always

Aaron Copland, the Best of Beethoven, and Mozart's Greatest Hits, and they would sometimes call down to me to turn it lower. I took off my jacket. If one was to be the seductive older woman one should probably not play it down.

He moved with authority through the records and tapes stacked by what I still referred to as the phonograph. "Why," Brynn always said, "do you think it's so cute to call it that? You know it's called a stereo. We don't want parents playing dumb."

"Hey, this is nice." Hedy picked up a Chuck Mangione album I really did like.

"Oh, I adore that," I said. Something in common.

As with the Fran Dorf example at the beginning of the chapter, there is wonderful dialogue in here—surrounded by so many beats, both internal and external, that its effect is lost. The fact that the beats themselves are interesting and well written doesn't keep the constant interruption from irritating the reader.

Some authors may overuse beats because they lack confidence in the ability of their dialogue to carry the story. After all, if you show every move your characters make, your readers are bound to be able to picture the action you describe. As in the following:

"Dad, have you seen the tickets to the concert tonight?"

Nancy caught me in the middle of doing the dinner dishes, one of my favorite times of day. There's something soothing in the slosh of the water, the smell of detergent, the shine of freshly washed plates. It's why I've never bought us a dishwasher.

"Weren't they over behind the toaster?" I scoured off a cookie sheet, ran it under the tap, and set it in the drying rack.

She grabbed the toaster and held it up, spraying bread crumbs on the counter. "Nope."

I sponged off a handful of butter knives, scraping a moment at a stubborn bit of crust. "Well, at the risk of sounding like a parent, where did you see them last."

"I don't know, that's why I'm asking."

I rinsed the knives, dropped them in the rack, and started on one of the plates. "I don't suppose you've asked your brother, have you."

She stared at me a moment, then said, "I'll kill him. I swear," and was gone before I could tell her to kill him quietly.

When you describe every bit of action down to the last detail, you give your readers a clear picture of what's going on, but the chances are good that you'll alienate them in the process. Describing your action too precisely can be as condescending as describing your characters' emotions. Far better to give your readers some hints and then allow them to fill in the blanks for themselves. Besides, when you interrupt dialogue too often, you keep your scenes from building. Eventually, your story will stutter to a halt.

On the other hand, page after page of uninterrupted dialogue can become disembodied and disorienting after a while, even if the dialogue itself is excellent. As in this passage from Toni Morrison's *The Bluest Eye*:

"What they going to do about Della? Don't she have no people?"

"A sister's coming up from North Carolina to look after her. I expect she wants to get ahold of Della's house."

"Oh, come on. That's an evil thought, if ever I heard one."

"What you want to bet? Henry Washington said that sister ain't seen Della in fifteen years."

"I kind of thought Henry would marry her one of these days."

"That old woman?"

"Well, Henry ain't no chicken."

"No, but he ain't no buzzard, either."

"He ever been married to anybody?"

"No."

"How come? Somebody cut it off?"

"He's just picky."

"He ain't picky. You see anything around here you'd marry?"

"Well...no."

"He's just sensible. A steady worker with quiet ways. I hope it works out all right."

"It will. How much you charging?"

"Five dollars every two weeks."

"That'll be a big help to you."

"I'll say."

Quite simply, the scene isn't as good as its dialogue. What's needed is a few beats to anchor it in reality. If you look back, you'll see that the edited version of the Fran Dorf example above still contains one beat ("I took off my glasses, rubbed my eyes.") and one snippet of interior monologue ("*An asylum?*"). As with narration/immediate scene, the idea is to strike the right balance between dialogue and beats.

So how do you know when and how often to include a beat? Well, as we said, beats allow your readers to picture your dialogue taking place. As with other forms of description, you want to give your readers enough detail to allow them to picture the action and yet enough leeway for their imaginations to work. You want to define the action without overdefining it. If your dialogue is taking place over dinner, for instance, an occasional dropped fork or sip of wine are enough to keep the readers on the scene. You don't need a description of the meal from soup to nuts.

You can also use beats to vary the rhythm of your dialogue. Uninterrupted dialogue not only becomes disembodied after a while, it becomes exhausting. Like a piece of good music, good dialogue has an ebb and flow to it. Where you want the tension high, as with the confrontation scene that opens this chapter, pare the beats down to a bare minimum. If you've just had two high-tension scenes in a row, let your readers relax a bit in the next one with some quiet conversation interspersed with pauses (signified by beats).

Notice how the beats in the following give a feel for the long, lazy pauses in the conversation:

"Hand me that, will you?"

Clem picked up a two-foot oak log and handed it over to me. I centered it on the chopping block, made sure it wasn't going to topple, and picked up the maul axe.

"So how much do you say you need?" I brought the axe down smartly, just off center on the log.

"No more than two hundred."

I levered the axe out of the log, brought it down again, sharp. Still no sign the log was going to give. I reached for the wedge.

Clem stepped back a bit. "Fact is, I can probably get along on one-fifty."

I tapped the wedge in a little, just enough so I knew it wouldn't bounce out, then hauled off and hit it one. "Clem, you're already into me for three-fifty. When am I going to see that?"

"Ed, this is going to work, I promise you."

I hit the wedge three more times, three sharp, ringing cracks, with a second, deep woody pop after the last one. Then, one final blow and the two halves of the log jumped off the block onto the piles on either side.

Although there are a lot of beats, the effect isn't interruptive. The action involved—the splitting of the stubborn log—acts as a counterpoint, almost a metaphor, for the dialogue. In other words the beats, though numerous, aren't pointless. Also, you can get away with more beats than usual when your characters are doing something few people are familiar with. Had these two characters been washing dishes or riding a bus instead of splitting a log, the number of beats would probably be too many.

The best way to fine-tune the rhythm of your dialogue, of course, is to read it aloud. Listen for the pauses as you read and if you find yourself pausing between two consecutive lines, insert a beat at that point.

Beats also serve to help define your characters. Any good actor knows the importance of body language in projecting a character and the same holds true in fiction. A few years ago, a

New York Times review complimented a new mystery on the quality of its characterization and demonstrated that quality by quoting a beat: "He blew his nose on the sheet." That little bit of action tells as much or more about that character than an entire page of narration on his slovenliness or even a description of his bedroom. Beats can be a powerful and efficient way to convey your characters.

They can also be pointless, distracting, cliched—or repetitive. Haven't you read scenes in which the characters are forever looking up, looking down, looking into each other's eyes, down at their hands, or out the window? You want to write beats that are as fresh, as unique, as your characters. No two people cross a room in the same way, and there are as many ways of showing, say, uneasiness as there are situations to make a character uneasy.

So where do you find good beats? Well, as Casey Stengel once said, you can see an awful lot just by looking. Watch your friends. Notice what they do with their hands when they're bored, with their legs when they're relaxed, with their eyes when they're nervous. Watch old movies—Bogart in particular used stage business very effectively. Watch yourself. Keep an eye open for those little movements that bring your personality to the surface, the gestures that reveal who you are or how you're feeling. If you collect enough of these little movements, your characters won't ever have to look at their hands again.

You can also see an awful lot just by reading. Start paying attention to beats as you read—the ones that make you wish you'd written them and the ones that distract or irritate. In the passages that follow, all of whose beats are in boldface type, you can absorb different authors' different ways of handling stage business.

You'll notice that good beats, as in this passage from Eudora Welty's story "The Wide Net," are unobtrusive:

> "I've lost Hazel, she's vanished, she went to drown herself."
> "Why, that ain't like Hazel," said Virgil.

William Wallace reached out and shook him. "You heard me. Don't you know we have to drag the river?"

"Right this minute?"

"You ain't got nothing to do till spring."

"Let me go set foot inside the house and speak to my mother and tell her a story, and I'll come back."

"This will take the wide net," said William Wallace.

His eyebrows gathered, and he was talking to himself.

The beat in the passage that follows, from Frederick Buechner's novel *Treasure Hunt*, supplies the all-important factor of the narrator's reaction to the dialogue:

"Of course [Mr. Bebb] raised me from the dead in Knoxville, Tennessee, dear. That was many years ago and you know the story. He was forever telling me he should have saved himself the trouble. He said I never really lived the life he'd gotten back for me, just shoved . . . just shoved it up my you-know-what and sat on it. He said hurtful things like that for my own good. He was my Rock of Gibraltar, and when he went, it seemed like he took my faith with him."

It was like driving past an accident. I tried not to look at Brownie as he spoke, but most of the time I couldn't help myself.

A longer beat can turn up the tension, as in this scene from John le Carré's *The Russia House*, in which the hero is undergoing intelligence grilling:

"Don't know a K, don't know a Katya, don't know a Yekaterina," Barley said. "Never screwed one, never flirted with one, never proposed to one, never even married one. Never *met* one, far as I remember. Yes, I did."

They waited, I waited; and we would have waited all night and there would not have been the creak of a chair or the clearing of a throat while Barley ransacked his memory for a Katya.

"Old cow in Aurora," Barley resumed. "Tried to flog me some art prints of Russian painters. I didn't bite. Aunts would have blown their corks."

"Aurora?" Clive asked, not knowing whether it was a city or a State agency.

"Publishers."

"Do you remember her other name?"

Barley shook his head, his face still out of sight. "Beard," he said. "Katya of the beard. Ninety in the shade."

A beat can also provide breathing space in an emotionally tense scene like the one from Ellen Gilchrist's *The Annunciation* in which the father of a child given up for adoption tells the mother he has seen their daughter:

"You went to look for her, didn't you?" Amanda said. "Tell me straight, Guy. I know you did. I know damn well that's what you were doing there."

"Let's go to your house," he said. "I don't want to talk about this in the car."

"Then stop the car," Amanda said.

He pulled the car over to the curb and turned and took her hands. "She looks like you. She's all right. She's married."

"What else?" Amanda said. "Tell me. Tell it all to me. She's blind, isn't she? I know she's blind. I've always known she would be blind. I remember when she was born her eyes were stuck together. I remember seeing them stuck together."

"She sees as good as you or me. She does everything. She was playing tennis. She won. I went to the New Orleans Lawn Tennis Club and watched her play."

"Then what is it?" Amanda said. "Tell me what you aren't telling me. Why do you sound like this?"

Guy turned his eyes away and let his hands drop from her arms. "She's very pretty and very ladylike and she's married to a young lawyer. You were right about one thing. If you'd kept on living there you would have met her sooner or later. You probably passed her on the street a thousand times."

"She looks like me?"

"Yes, but with dark hair. She's quieter. Well, I don't know that. I didn't get to talk to her. I just watched her play tennis. I kept thinking she looked like Grandmomma might have when she was young."

"She won?"

"Of course," he said. "Of course she won."

In a powerful, poignant scene from Anne Tyler's *Dinner at the Homesick Restaurant*, the beats accomplish both purposes simultaneously—increased tension and breathing space:

"And see what I was like at your age?" **She handed him the picture with the tam-o'shanter.**

He glanced over. He frowned. He said, "Who did you say that was?"

"Me."

"No, it's not."

"Yes, it is. Me at thirteen. Mother wrote the date on the back."

"It's not!" he said. **His voice was unusually high; he sounded like a much younger child.** "It isn't! Look at it! Why, it's like a . . . concentration camp person, a victim, Anne Frank. It's terrible! It's so sad!"

Surprised, she turned the photo around and looked again.

"So what?" she asked, **and she held it out to him once more. He drew back sharply.**

"It's somebody else," he told her. "Not you; you're always laughing and having fun. It's not you."

"Oh, fine, it's not me, then," she said, **and she returned to the rest of the photos.**

For the sake of contrast, take a look at the same scene with the beats eliminated:

"And see what I was like at your age?"

He said, "Who did you say that was?"

"Me."

"No, it's not."

"Yes, it is. Me at thirteen. Mother wrote the date on the back."

"It's not! It isn't! Look at it! Why, it's like a . . . concentration camp person, a victim, Anne Frank! It's terrible! It's so sad!"

"So what?"

"It's somebody else," he told her. "Not you; you're always laughing and having fun. It's not you."

"Oh, fine, it's not me, then," she said.

The scene is still moving—the dialogue effectively conveys what's going on and its importance, and it's easy to tell who is speaking. What's lost is a great deal of the resonance, the deepening of the emotional content.

CHECKLIST

• How many beats do you have?. (It may be time to get out the highlighters yet again and mark all your beats.) How often do you interrupt your dialogue?

• What are your beats describing? Familiar, everyday actions (such as dialing a telephone or buying groceries)? How often do you repeat a beat? Are your characters always looking out of windows or lighting cigarettes? (Garrison Keillor said of his first novel, "My characters smoked cigarettes the way some people use semicolons.")

• Do your beats help illuminate your characters? Are they individual or general actions anyone might take under just about any circumstances?

• Do your beats fit the rhythm of your dialogue? Read it aloud and find out.

EXERCISES

A. First, try editing out beats that don't work.

"You're sure it runs?" Mr. Dietz said.

I leaned against the fender. "It did last time I tried it."

"Yeah, well, when was that." He peered through the back window.

I picked at some dirt under my fingernails. "Just last week. Here, listen." I pulled out the key, hopped in the front seat, inserted the key, drew the choke, popped it into neutral, and hit the starter. The engine ground a few times, caught, and then sputtered and died. I pumped the gas once or twice and tried again. This time it caught and began to purr.

"Well, I don't know. It sounds all right, but I don't like the looks of the body." He kicked the tire.

"Look, for three hundred dollars, what do you want?" I pulled the hood release, stepped around to the front, and lifted the hood. "I mean, listen to that, it's running like a baby. You should get twenty thousand miles out of this with no trouble. At least twenty."

He peered into one of the wheel wells. "As long as one of the tires doesn't fall off on me."

I slammed the hood. "There's a spare in the trunk. Now what do you say."

B. Now for one where you have to put the beats in.

"Do you really think this is a smart move?" she said. "I mean, you don't know anybody in California."

"I'm pretty sure," he said. "After all, it's not as if I have a choice. You've got to go where the jobs are."

"What about the kids?"

"Honey, it's not like I'm going to be gone forever. I'll send for you as soon as I can."

"Yeah, but when will that be? Where are you going to stay, what are you going to do, how are you going to live there?"

"I'm taking the tent, and I can sleep in the car if need be. Besides, I'll find something within a week, I'll bet you."

"I . . . it's just that I'm scared."

"I know. So am I."

···

CHAPTER 8

BREAKING UP
IS EASY TO DO

Read through the following confrontation between a talk-show host and his guest:

> In the final few moments, Curtin had pulled what he probably considered his trump card, laying the blame for every problem in Vietnamese life on the war. (On the American war, long over, Bernie pointed out, not the decade of war afterward against Cambodia. And not, surely not, on the vast portion of the Vietnamese budget currently going into the military. "Somewhere between forty and fifty percent, isn't it?" Bernie had asked pleasantly. Pat Curtin had blinked). Is it, Bernie then asked, "that America should feel so guilty for Hanoi's every brutality, every rigidity, every mismanagement, that we will rush to follow diplomatic recognition with reparations and foreign aid and trade and

investment and—what else? Delegations of unpaid experts? Planeloads of privileged college kids, eager to play at work they know they can walk away from?" Curtin's mouth had tightened and Bernie, a veteran debater, had smelled the panic of a cornered animal. Time for the kill.

Now read the passage as edited:

"Finally," Curtin said, "one must realize that the vast majority of problems today all come back to the war."

"The American war, you mean?" Bernie had said.

"Of course."

"Not the decade of war against Cambodia?"

"Well, that—"

"And surely not on the vast portion of the Vietnamese budget currently going into the military. Somewhere between forty and fifty percent, isn't it?"

"They *have* to spend—"

"Is it," Bernie said, "that America should feel so guilty for Hanoi's every brutality, every rigidity, every mismanagement, that we will rush to follow diplomatic recognition with reparations and foreign aid and trade and investment and—what else? Delegations of unpaid experts? Planeloads of privileged college kids, eager to play at work they know they can walk away from?"

Curtin's mouth had tightened and Bernie, a veteran debater, had smelled the panic of a cornered animal.

Time for the kill.

You probably noticed that the first version tells, where showing would be more effective—the author narrates bits of the interview that belong in dialogue. But another editing technique produces the dramatic difference between the two versions: the first is a single, page-long paragraph; the second has been broken up into more manageable chunks. The second has white space.

At the beginning of *Alice in Wonderland*, Alice glances at a book her sister is reading, notices that it has no pictures or conversations, and thinks, "And what is the use of a book without pictures or conversations." If you've ever leafed though a book in a bookstore and noticed page after page of long, dense paragraphs, you probably know how Alice felt. Before you've read a word, you're turned off.

So be on the lookout for paragraphs that run more than, say, a half-page in length. Whether it's because readers feel lectured to, or because they feel crowded, or simply because some white space on the page is visually inviting, lengthy unbroken chunks of written material are off-putting. The simple, purely mechanical change of paragraphing more frequently can make your writing much more engaging.

Paragraphing frequently can also add tension to a scene. In the example above, although the dialogue was all there in the single paragraph, it didn't convey the tension between the two men until it was edited into a series of rapid-fire questions followed by two- and three-word answers. Whether it's because sentences tend to grow shorter as the speakers become more upset, or simply because readers' eyes move down the page more quickly, frequent paragraphs give dialogue snap and momentum.

Many authors who write thrillers seem to use this technique instinctively. Consider this passage from Elmore Leonard's *La Brava*:

La Brava said, "You know the big blond guy."

"The Silver Kid," Paco said, "of course."

"I want somebody to deliver a note to him, at his hotel."

"Sure."

"And write it."

"What does it say?"

"I want him to come to the park tonight, 1:00 A.M., across from the Play House Bar."

"Sign your name?"

"No, sign it C.R."

"Just C.R.?"

"That's the *Marielito*, the one with the earring."

"The Publisher has asked Granville to be on the lookout for paragraphs that run more than a half page in length."

"Oh," Paco said, "yes, I remember."

"But I have to make sure the big blond guy gets the message and not the police."

Paco said, "Man, you got something going on."

"If I can, I'd like to get hold of a baseball bat," La Brava said. "But I think the stores are closed."

"You and this guy going to play ball? In the dark? Never mind, don't tell me," Paco said. "I got one for softball, you can use."

"I'll take good care of it," La Brava said.

Not that you're going to want to maintain this sort of pace for very long. A novel that is literally a page-turner beginning to end is more likely to leave its readers feeling weary—and manipulated—than satisfied. When you want to create a more relaxed mood, or give your readers a chance to breathe (or reflect), or simply lull them into complacency before you spring something on them, try paragraphing a little less frequently than usual. John le Carré uses the technique to great effect in *The Secret Pilgrim:*

> Two armchairs stood before a dying fire. One was empty. I took it to be the Professor's. In the other, somewhat obscured from my line of sight, sat a silky, rounded man of forty with a cap of soft black hair and twinkling round eyes that said we were all friends, weren't we? His winged chair was high-backed and he had fitted himself into the angle of it like an aircraft passenger prepared for landing. His rather circular shoes stopped short of the floor, and it occurred to me they were East European shoes: marbled, of an uncertain leather, with moulded, heavy-treaded soles. His hairy brown suit was like a remodeled military uniform. Before him stood a table with a pot of mauve hyacinths on it, and beside the hyacinths lay a display of objects which I recognised as the instruments of silent killing: two garottes made of wooden toggles and lengths of piano wire; a screwdriver so sharpened that it was a stiletto; a Charter Arms .38 Undercover revolver with a five-shot cylinder, together with two kinds of bullet, six soft-nosed and six rifled, with congealed powder squashed into the grooves.
>
> "It is cyanide," the Professor explained, in answer to my silent perplexity.

The leisurely tone and seemingly innocuous, soft-edged details help lull the reader into a relaxed moment—to a purpose, since we are being set up. But what greatly supports this aim is the author's use of a long paragraph, in effect keeping us in that chair until he's ready to spring the cyanide on us.

You can also focus attention on some important development by placing it in its own, short paragraph. Consider this chapter ending from *Down Will Come Baby*, a tense novel of psychological suspense, by Gloria Murphy:

[Amelia is thirteen, drunk, and drowning. Robin has just swum out to rescue her.]

"Stop it!" Robin screamed, but Amelia was too terrified to hear her. She pounced on Robin's back, her arms clasped tightly around her neck, and dragged her down. Robin fought to free herself, but it was as though strong tentacles were pulling her deeper and deeper.

It wasn't until she swallowed the second mouthful of water that Robin stopped the struggle. Then slowly, slowly, wrapped together like sleeping Siamese twins, they began to drift upward. When they finally broke the surface, Robin took a gasp of air, turned, swung her arm out, and bashed Amelia in the face. Amelia let go.

Robin—choking and gagging, barely able to tread water—watched as Amelia sank for the last time, her eyes all the while pleading with Robin not to let her die.

Now try this version:

"Stop it!" Robin screamed, but Amelia was too terrified to hear her. She pounced on Robin's back, her arms clasped tightly around her neck, and dragged her down. Robin fought to free herself, but it was as though strong tentacles were pulling her deeper and deeper.

It wasn't until she swallowed the second mouthful of water that Robin stopped the struggle. Then slowly, slowly, wrapped together like sleeping Siamese twins, they began to drift upward. When they finally broke the surface, Robin took a gasp of air, turned, swung her arm out, and bashed Amelia in the face.

Amelia let go.

The first version was well-written and exciting. But the second, by focusing all the horror of Amelia's death into that single, three-word paragraph, ends the chapter with a dramatic punch that the first version lacks. And the only difference between the two is the extra paragraph and the cut.

When you reread a scene or chapter for self-editing, be on

the lookout for places where your characters make little speeches to one another. In formal dialogue, characters often string together four or five complete, well-formed sentences. In real life, few of us get that far without interruption. So break your dialogue up, write in more give-and-take between your characters, have your characters interrupt one another—and themselves. Let them mix it up a little, or a lot.

But sometimes it's *appropriate* for the character to make a speech, in which case a long paragraph may be effective. In the scene quoted in the last chapter from Frederick Buechner's *Treasure Hunt,* Brownie has told the narrator that he never really lived the life Bebb gave him back and so has lost his faith. Following the little speech he makes about that—a speech the author wisely leaves in one piece—the give-and-take of *dialogue* reasserts itself, all the more effectively for Brownie's having been allowed to spill over:

> He said, "Another thing. I have carnal desires like everybody else, dear. Maybe you wouldn't believe it to look at me, but I've had many opportunities for backsliding in that direction here on the ranch. These Indians, they don't mean any harm by it, but lots of times they don't care a fig what they do or who they do it with just as long as they get a chance to do it. It's like when you've got a healthy young appetite, you'll take anything that's put before you. I've always resisted these temptations because of my faith. I've passed up things that . . . joys . . . ." He took off his glasses and rubbed his eyes with his thumb and forefinger. He said, "Now I ask myself this question. All these precious things I've given up for Jesus, what have I got to show for it?"
>
> I said, "Brownie, your interpretations of scripture bring lots of people comfort and hope."
>
> He said, "Scripture says, 'Cast thy bread upon the waters for thou shalt find it after many days.' I have cast my whole life upon the waters, and it's sunk out of sight like a stone."
>
> "Nobody knows you've lost your faith, Brownie. You can keep on helping people anyway. That way you might get it back again."

He said, "You don't know how it feels to say things you don't believe any more. It's like a woman with a dead baby inside her."

In *I Never Promised You a Rose Garden*, Hannah Green puts the theme of the novel into the mouth of her psychiatrist, suddenly confronted by her patient's awareness of injustice within the "safe" world of the mental hospital—and gives it its own paragraph:

"Helene kept her bargain about Ellis and so did I," Deborah said. "What good is your reality then?"

"Look here," Furii said. "I never promised you a rose garden. I never promised you perfect justice...[or] peace or happiness. My help is so that you can be free to fight for all of these things. The only reality I offer is challenge, and being well is being free to accept it or not at whatever level you are capable. I never promise lies, and the rose-garden world of perfection is a lie . . . and a bore, too!"

"Will you bring it up at the meeting—about Helene?"

"I said I would and I will, but I promise nothing."

And in this passage from *Dinner at the Homesick Restaurant*, you can see how the author uses both short and long paragraphs for effect in the same scene. Anne Tyler surrounds two spillover speeches—by a father and son who haven't seen each other in twenty-five years—with a series of one-line paragraphs:

"You left us in her clutches," Cody said.

Beck looked up. He said, "Huh?"

"How could you do that?" Cody asked him. "How could you just dump us on our mother's mercy?" He bent closer, close enough to smell the camphorish scent of Beck's suit. "We were kids, we were only kids, we had no way of protecting ourselves. We looked to you for help. We listened for your step at the door so we'd be safe, but you just turned your back on us. You didn't lift a finger to defend us."

Beck stared past Cody at the traffic.

"She wore me out," he told Cody finally.

"Wore you out?"

"Used up my good points. Used up all my good points."

Cody straightened.

"Oh, at the start," Beck said, "she thought I was wonderful. You ought to have seen her face when I walked into a room. When I met her, she was an old maid already. She'd given up. No one had courted her for years, her girlfriends were asking her to baby-sit, their children called her Aunt Pearl. Then I came along. I made her so happy! There's my downfall, son, I just can't resist a person I make happy. I expect if I'd got that divorce from your mother I'd have married six times over, just moving on to each new woman that cheered up some when she saw me, moving on again when she got close to me and didn't act so pleased any more. Oh, it's closeness that does you in. Never get too close to people, son—did I tell you that when you were little? When your mother and I were first married, everything was perfect. It seemed I could do no wrong. Then bit by bit I guess she saw my faults. I'd never hid them, but now it seemed they mattered after all. She saw that I was away from home too much, didn't get ahead in my work, put on weight, talked wrong, dressed wrong, drove a car wrong. I'd bring home a simple toy, say, and it would somehow start a fight—your mother saying it was too expensive or too dangerous, and the three of you kids bickering over who got to play with it first...."

Up until now, we've talked about breaking your writing up on the level of paragraphs. But it's also a good idea to break your writing up on a larger scale. If you have a single scene that runs fifteen or twenty pages (or more), it may be more effective broken up into two scenes. The same holds true for chapters that run on for, say, twenty-five or more pages.

These figures are a little arbitrary, of course—some authors are capable of sustaining their readers' interest through scenes that run many times the usual chapter length of ten to twenty pages. But for most fiction writers, most of the time, the principle is sound. By varying the rhythm of what you offer the reader, you make it more engaging. If you also use paragraphing as an "engaging" technique, variety will pay off there as well.

CHECKLIST

• Flip through your manuscript without even reading it—just notice the white space. How much of it is there? Do you have any paragraphs that go on more than a page in length?

• Do you have chapters with large, clunky paragraphs, more than, say, ten lines in length?

• If one of your scenes seems to drag, try paragraphing a little more often.

• Do you have scenes with *no* longer paragraphs? Remember, what you're after is the right balance.

• Have your characters made little speeches to one another?

EXERCISES

A. Read through the opening of this Garrison Keillor story from Leaving Home, *first as written; then broken up into two, then into four paragraphs. Notice the different effect the same passage has on the reader with only the paragraphing changed:*

It has been a quiet week in Lake Wobegon. Sunday morning

Clarence Bunsen stepped into the shower and turned on the

water—which was cold, but he's Norwegian, he knows you have to

take what you get—and stood until it got warm, and was reaching

for the soap when he thought for sure he was having a heart attack.

He's read a *Reader's Digest* story about a man's heart attack ("My

Most Unforgettable Experience") and this felt like the one in the story—chest pain like a steel band tightening. Clarence grabbed the nozzle as the rest of the story flashed before his eyes: the ride in the ambulance, the dash to the emergency room, unconsciousness as the heart team worked over him, the long slow recovery and the discovery of a new set of values. But as he imagined what was about to happen, the heart attack petered out on him. The story said it felt like an elephant stepping on you. This felt more like a big dog, and then somebody whistled and the dog left. So it wasn't a heart attack, there was no story, and Clarence felt better.

It has been a quiet week in Lake Wobegon. Sunday morning Clarence Bunsen stepped into the shower and turned on the water—which was cold, but he's Norwegian, he knows you have to take what you get—and stood until it got warm, and was reaching for the soap when he thought for sure he was having a heart attack. He's read a *Reader's Digest* story about a man's heart attack ("My Most Unforgettable Experience") and this felt like the one in the story—chest pain like a steel band tightening.

Clarence grabbed the nozzle as the rest of the story flashed before his eyes: the ride in the ambulance, the dash to the emergency room, unconsciousness as the heart team worked over him, the long slow recovery and the discovery of a new set of values. But as he imagined what was about to happen, the heart attack petered out on him. The story said it felt like an elephant stepping on you. This felt more like a big dog, and then somebody whistled and the dog left. So it wasn't a heart attack, there was no story, and Clarence felt better.

It has been a quiet week in Lake Wobegon.

Sunday morning Clarence Bunsen stepped into the shower and turned on the water—which was cold, but he's Norwegian, he knows you have to take what you get—and stood until it got warm, and was reaching for the soap when he thought for sure he was having a heart attack. He's read a *Reader's Digest* story about a man's heart attack ("My Most Unforgettable Experience") and this felt like the one in the story—chest pain like a steel band tightening.

Clarence grabbed the nozzle as the rest of the story flashed

before his eyes: the ride in the ambulance, the dash to the emer-

gency room, unconsciousness as the heart team worked over him,

the long slow recovery and the discovery of a new set of values.

But as he imagined what was about to happen, the heart

attack petered out on him. The story said it felt like an elephant

stepping on you. This felt more like a big dog, and then somebody

whistled and the dog left.

So it wasn't a heart attack, there was no story, and Clarence

felt better.

You may find (as do we) that the version which appeals most to you is the second one—in which the material is broken up just enough to render it easier to follow but not enough to damage the flavor of what is, after all, a radio monologue. The point is, the content of the paragraph hasn't changed by so much as one word; the effect *has*.

Now look back over a scene or chapter of your own and select a paragraph—of narration, dialogue, interior monologue—that runs at least fifteen lines. (If none qualifies, run two longish paragraphs together for purposes of the exercise.) Experiment with paragraphing and compare the effects when it is broken up frequently, occasionally, or not at all.

B. *Read through this passage and note where you might paragraph it differently (be warned, the changes that will make a difference are subtle:*

Jeannine stared at the spider plant hung over the kitchen sink. Most of its leaves were yellow and a few were going brown at the edges. "I don't believe this," she said.

"What?" Ed said.

"I only gave you this plant a month ago, and look at it now." She reached out and tenderly touched one of the leaves. It came off in her hand. "I mean, this is a spider plant. You can't kill these things, they thrive on neglect. How did you manage to do this much damage so quickly?" She stuck one finger in the potting soil.

"I don't know. I've been watering it once a week, just like you said. I've even been using plant food I picked up at the hardware store the other day. It's that blue powder that dissolves in water, one tablespoon to the quart."

"Ed, let me see that plant food." He opened the cupboard under the sink, rummaged around for a moment, and came up with a box with a picture of a rose on front. She took it and scanned the instructions. "According to this, you're supposed to use one teaspoon to the quart."

"Oh, well, I guess that explains it then."

....

CHAPTER 9

ONCE IS USUALLY ENOUGH

[D]espite its tireless narrative energy, despite its relentless inventiveness, the book is bloated, grown to elephantine proportions . . . . Repetition is the problem; the same stories are told several times, accruing more detail with each telling. Also, the principal characters have a way of regurgitating what they've learned, even though the reader was with them when they learned it.

—PATRICK MCGRATH, in a *New York Times* review of *The Witching Hour* by Anne Rice

The problem Mr. McGrath has picked up on is one we see regularly in the writing of both novices and professionals: unintentional repetition. Most authors already know to edit out places where they have literally repeated a word or phrase. But the repetition of an *effect* can be just as problematic. Whether it's two sentences that convey the same information, two paragraphs that establish the same personality trait, or two characters who fill the same role in the plot, repetition can dissipate your writing and rob it of its power.

Even experienced authors have occasional trouble with repetition, usually because they're too close to what they've accomplished with their writing to spot the places where they've accomplished it twice. But more often the problem shows up in the fiction of novices. The reason is a lack of confidence on the author's part. After all, it takes quite a bit of experience and insight to judge exactly what effect your writing will have on your readers. So when you have a character point or plot development that is critical to the story, you want to make sure the readers get it and so you may drive it home in several different ways.

But chances are good that you've underestimated your readers' intelligence, or your own writing ability, or both. As a result, you wind up telling your readers things they already know, which is almost as condescending (and off-putting) as describing emotions that have already been shown in the dialogue. Consider the following:

> By this time, Jerry wished he could bring his Mustang to his father's garage near Tralee. He missed his father's garage. It was a small, cluttered shop off the main road, and sometimes he ached to be there. He remembered throwing down his books after school and running back to the garage to do a little "jobeen" for his father. Picking his way through the parts, handing his father particular wrenches, listening to his dad's Irish names for parts of the car: *roth* for wheel, *coisceain* for brakes, *inneal* for engine. He remembered especially his father's Irish phrase for carburetor: *croi an innill*, the heart of the engine, the heart of the machine. He missed all this, and wondered why he'd ever left.

Here the author is trying too hard to impress us with how much Jerry misses his father's garage—we're told about it no less than three times. The author doesn't have to tell us even once. The description *shows* how much Jerry misses the place, as you can see from a version with the repetitions removed:

> By this time, Jerry wished he could bring his Mustang to his father's garage near Tralee, the small, cluttered shop off the main road where he used to throw down his books after school and run in to do a little "jobeen" for his father. Pick his way through the parts, hand his father particular wrenches, learn his dad's Irish names for parts of the car: *roth* for wheel, *coisceain* for brakes, *inneal* for engine. He remembered especially his father's phrase for carburetor: *croi an innill*, the heart of the engine, the heart of the machine.

Besides the condescension involved, repeating an effect simply doesn't work. In fact, repetition is likely to weaken rather than intensify the power of that effect. Take a look at this excerpt from a dinner scene:

> "It's enough just to be here. With you." She took his hands in hers and played with them while she talked. "We can be by ourselves later, we can make love and sleep and make more love—later. Right now this is all I can hold."
>
> It was enough for him, too. He feasted on the sight of her taking big bites of the veal, washing them down with long, long swallows of wine.
>
> By the time the second course had been served, she was pronouncing her words very, very carefully. And when she excused herself to go to the ladies' room, she kept bumping into the tables to the right and left of her.

Notice that the author conveys the heroine's inebriation in two ways—the careful pronunciation and the staggering. But the staggering (which is a cliché) tends to undermine the careful pronunciation (which is fresher and more effective). Because when you try to accomplish the same effect twice, the weaker attempt is likely to undermine the power of the stronger one. Inspired by a very gifted novelist-client who is also a gifted writing instructor, we often write a formula in the margin of manuscripts: $1 + 1 = 1/2$.

Or take another example, this one lifted from one of our favorite five-page workshop submissions:

> [Rita is the narrator's oldest friend. She is also a ghost.]
> There are times I'm glad no one but me sees Rita, like when we hit the bars. In spite of her size, Rita still thinks of herself as a sexy broad. She wears long dangling gold earrings, or rhinestone baubles that twinkle too much to pass for the real thing. And she shows too much bust. Now when you weigh almost two hundred pounds, any bust is too much in my opinion, but Rita doesn't see it that way. I guess it goes with her tiger-striped dresses and red hair. Now I know you're thinking, why should a spook have dyed hair? But who am I to deny the black roots in Rita's coiffure?

The author conveys Rita's habit of gaudy dress three times, and although each instance reads delightfully, the cumulative effect is still to weaken the whole—as can be seen from a look at the passage with the one-plus-ones edited out:

> There are times I'm glad no one but me sees Rita, like when we hit the bars. She wears long dangling gold earrings, and she shows too much bust. Now, when you weigh two hundred pounds, any bust showing is too much in my opinion, but Rita doesn't see it that way. I guess it goes with her tiger-striped dresses and dyed red hair.
> I don't expend any energy wondering why a ghost should have dyed hair—who am I to deny Rita's roots?

One form of repetition that we've seen more often in recent years is the use of brand names to help characterization. The mention of what type of scotch your hero drinks or what kind of car your heroine drives may help give your readers a handle on their personalities. But when all your characters glance at their Rolexes, then hop in their Maseratis to tear out to the house in the Hamptons, where they change into their Armanis and pour themselves a Glenlivet—you've gone too far. You don't want to sound as though you used a Sharper Image catalogue for a thesaurus.

We once worked on a manuscript in which the hero drove a Porsche Targa. Evidently this was the author's dream car, because he mentioned it every chance he got. After forty or fifty pages of "hopping in the Targa," and "taking the Targa to the Hendrick's," and "running the Targa out to Long Island," one of our editors took to writing "Just call it the car!" in the margins.

Interior monologue is also prone to needless repetition, possibly because our thoughts tend to run in circles when we're upset. And sometimes you can capture a character's mood by showing his or her thoughts chasing their tails. But more often than not, repetition in interior monologue is like rambling, repetitive dialogue—authentic, but tedious. Consider this passage taken from an unpublished novel in which the heroine's lover and (her) children have left the campsite—and the heroine:

What was the matter with her? What was stopping her from stopping *them*? All she had to do was say she was sorry—for something, for anything—to make it all right, have him come back and hold her, hold them all in his large embrace. *I'm sorry for . . .* What?

She looked at the packet of dried milk that lay on the ground and couldn't think of one single thing to be sorry for. She stirred the damned ground turkey, which would remain tasteless no matter how much garlic she put in it and which now nobody would eat and which she would not throw away no matter how much she hated it. She could never bring herself to waste anything. She was a saver, a keeper, had kept herself and the children all those first years, alone.

Now read the passage with the one-plus-ones pared down to ones, and you can see that the interior monologue takes on a new strength. Notice especially the power of the last line, which in the unedited version was all but effaced by the sentence that preceded it:

> What was stopping her from stopping *them*? All she had to do was say she was sorry to make it all right, make him come back and hold her, hold them all in his large embrace. *I'm sorry for . . .* What?
>
> She looked at the packet of dried milk that lay broken at her feet and couldn't think of one single thing to be sorry for. She stirred the damned ground turkey, which would remain tasteless no matter how much garlic she put in it and which she would not throw away no matter how much she hated it. She was a saver, a keeper, had kept herself and the children all those first years, alone.

Incidentally, note that the phrase "on the ground" has been changed to "at her feet" because the ground of the campsite and the ground turkey are only a sentence apart. Keep an eye out for unconscious repetitions on the smallest scale—especially repetitions in which the repeated word isn't used in the same sense as the original word. ("She heard a sharp crack, then the loud spring of her bedsprings.")

But also note: in the campsite passage above, "stopping," "make," "hold," and "sorry" are all repeated, and to good effect. There is also deliberate (and effective) repetition in the three phrases strung together about the fate of the ground turkey. A fringe benefit of getting rid of unnecessary repetitions is that it frees up the power of intentional repetitions, or repetitions for effect.

You may want to repeat an effect because your plot point or character attribute is so subtle or powerful that it pays to approach it from two different directions. Or you may use different approaches to the same point to introduce new insights, a literary version of the cinematic *Rashomon* technique.

And your repetition for effect will be that much stronger once the needless repetitions are removed.

Finally, to show that reviewers notice repetition problems as well, consider this from a review by Carolyn See of Tim Paulson's *The Real World*:

> This is a paean to dullness and inattention to detail. . . . So what if on Page 117 Tom's sister "hams up" her Southern accent and on Page 119 Mac Stuart "hams up" a Southern accent? So what if on Page 334, after Tom and Julie move to Brooklyn, "their *real friends* braved the three subway transfers" and on Page 335 Tom remarks: "We found out who our *real friends* are when they come to see us?" This is the real world, for Pete's sake! And whoever said the real world was anything more than dull, repetitive, and boring?

Up until now, we've been talking about small-scale repetition—repeating an effect two or more times within a scene or chapter. But as you revise, be on the lookout for unwarranted repetition on the larger scale as well. When you write two or more chapters that accomplish the same thing, or when you have two or more characters who fill the same role in the story, you dissipate your writing just as much as when you have two sentences or paragraphs that accomplish the same thing. On all scales, it's better to do it once and do it well than to do it twice.

We once worked with an author whose hero was being stalked by a person or persons unknown for reasons equally unknown. In the process of discovering who was trying to kill him and why, the hero received help from a buddy from Vietnam, an old school friend, the friend's wife (who had Mafia connections), and a Mafia don. The plot was already well supplied with characters, and now here were four more, all of them being put to essentially the same purpose.

We suggested character-combining, and the author liked the idea. When he was done, the old school friend and his wife were gone, the Vietnam buddy and the Mafia don had taken over the wife's and friend's part in the plot, and the story was easier to follow and more fun to read. The author had, in effect, been using four characters to do the work of two.

"Wendele's hero is being stalked by a person
or persons unknown for reasons equally unknown…"

While you're looking at the big picture, bear in mind that there are some effects that will work no more than once in an entire novel. Having your hero become sick to his stomach can be a good way to show he is upset, for instance. But *Spy* magazine once collected all of the passages from Julia Phillips' *You'll Never Eat Lunch in This Town Again* in which her characters threw up for various reasons. After reading all these passages in a row (and there were about twenty of them), you were glad you never had to eat lunch in Hollywood.

Another way in which authors indulge in large-scale overkill is in the creation of characters. When you're trying to create a distinctive or eccentric character, it's not hard to go over the line into stereotype or cartoon. We once worked with an author on a suspense novel that involved a serial killer in a college town in the midwest. The killer and the police chief tracking him were well-drawn characters of considerable depth; the murders, truly harrowing. The author decided he needed some comic relief, for which purpose he added a foolish college president, a vain trustee, a militant student, and a dim-witted custodian. Since all four of these characters were more cartoons than flesh and blood, they stuck out against the backdrop of realistically drawn characters. Their purpose in the story was obvious, and a good idea (the novel *did* need some comic relief) was undone by overkill.

Again, when you overdo some aspect of your novel for effect, the effect you are likely to get may be just the opposite of the one you intended. This is particularly true in the creation of heavies. Far too often, fictional antagonists are so thoroughly evil, so rapacious or sadistic or vain, that they actually cease to be frightening. The most frightening heavies, of course, are those readers can understand and identify with on some level—perhaps even imagine ourselves becoming in the right circumstances. Cartoons, even evil cartoons, aren't nearly as frightening as real human beings.

A suspense novelist who uses this principle to striking effect is Gloria Murphy. The antagonist in *Nightshade* kidnaps a woman's two children and holds them hostage to attract her to a cabin in the Maine woods. Once there, she discovers his true purpose: to have the family he always wanted and never had. The man is a psychopath, and his pathology is truly frightening—years earlier, he murdered the woman's first husband and raped her—but he's also a character we can identify with on some level. After all, the only thing he wants is a family of his own.

Then there is repetition on the largest scale, from book to book. We once worked with an author on an unusual, well-written novel about a rich, upper class gentlemen in San Francisco who falls in love with a dirt-poor, endearing Chinese woman. Their love affair, having destroyed his marriage and career, eventually breaks apart thanks to incompatibilities between the lovers' eastern and western sensibilities.

As developed, the theme and plot are wonderfully engaging. But in the author's second novel, a passionate love affair between a rich westerner and a charming Japanese woman eventually breaks up thanks to east/west incompatibility. And at the heart of the third book lies a romance between a rich westerner and a Korean woman . . . you get the picture.

Of course, there is room in the world of fiction for the formulaic novel—it's been said that every James Bond novel has the same plot. But when you repeat the same character under different names in several of your novels, or invoke the same clever plot twist more than once, you are weakening the effectiveness of what you've created just at the point where you want most to be original.

Many of the self-editing points in this book reflect changes in stylistic fashion—beginning, if you recall, with showing and telling. But the "once is (usually) enough" principle has apparently been valid for over a century. Consider this from Mark Twain's review of James Fenimore Cooper's Leatherstocking novels:

> . . . In his little box of stage properties [Cooper] kept six or eight cunning devices, tricks, artifices for his savages and woodsmen to deceive and circumvent each other with, and he was never so happy as when he was working these innocent things and seeing them go. A favorite one was to make a moccasined person tread in the tracks of the moccasined enemy, and thus hide his own trail. Cooper wore out barrels and barrels of moccasins in working that trick. Another stage-property that he pulled out of his box pretty frequently was his broken twig. . . . It is a restful chapter in any book of his when somebody doesn't step on a dry twig and alarm all the reds and whites for two hundred yards around. Every time a Cooper person is in peril, and absolute silence is worth four dollars a minute, he is sure to step on a dry twig. . . . In fact, the Leather Stocking Series ought to have been called the Broken Twig Series.

CHECKLIST

• Reread your manuscript, keeping in mind what you are trying to do with each paragraph—what character point you're trying to establish, what sort of mood you're trying to create, what background you're trying to suggest. In how many different ways are you accomplishing each of these ends?

• If more than one way, try reading the passage without the weakest approach and see if it isn't more effective.

• How about on the chapter level? Do you have more than one chapter that accomplishes the same thing?

• Is there a plot device or stylistic effect you are particularly pleased with? How often do you use it?

• Are your villains villainous in more than one way? Have you given them any characteristics that will allow your readers to sympathize with them?

• Finally, keep on the lookout for unintentional word repeats. Remember, the more striking a word or phrase is, the more jarring it will be if you repeat it.

EXERCISES
A. Trim the repetition out of the following:

"Come on in, don't be bashful."

It wasn't exactly bashfulness that was keeping me in the hall-

way. This was my first visit to a bachelor's apartment, and I was

shocked at how much it lived up to the reputation. It wasn't just

the velvet painting of Elvis on the wall above the blue velvet couch, or the orange shag rug, or the formica coffee table, or the wall unit that looked like it was made of genuine simulated plastic wood. It was the sense that the place had been lived in, and lived in hard.

There were nicks in the top of the coffee table that looked as if they might have been caused by tap shoes. There was also a small collection of cigarette burns on one arm of the dark brown vinyl recliner in front of the TV. The TV antenna was a bent coathanger with an undershirt hanging from it. Presumably a dirty undershirt—I didn't want to get close enough to check. Also, there were one or two unidentified stains on the ceiling.

"Like it?" he said. "I spent all day yesterday cleaning it up, just for you."

B. *Then there's this description, from an early draft of* A Reasonable Madness *by Fran Dorf:*

Clancy is a referral from Marilyn Reinhold via Donald Grayson via Rose Sumner. Frankly, I'm ashamed of my colleagues, passing the man around that way, not that I don't understand it. It's just that Clancy's so damned *boring*. I guess my colleagues feel there

are so many interesting people in this city who get into therapy—homosexual television producers, actresses sleeping their
way to the top, hot shot ad agency heads, philandering Wall
Street dynamos—that it's not necessary to suffer through a
patient like Clancy. It *is* tempting to turn him away, I've thought
about it myself. Clancy's an accountant for a small rock salt distributor in Queens. He's a pale and timid man with a vapid smile
and a nasal, rambling speaking style, so slow you could fall asleep
before he gets the next word out. Particularly annoying is his
undying allegiance to his employer of ten years who pays him at
the end of that loyal service the great sum of $22,000 per year,
and who expects overtime without pay on a consistent basis.
Clancy's really a very nice man, but his problems are small,
small, and boring.

CHAPTER 10

PROPORTION

Eammon flung the peavey to shore, reached down, and lifted Sunshine by grabbing his jacket collar with his left hand and his belt with his rig ht hand. He then spun around, clutching the Indian's left shoulder, leaned down to put his right shoulder into Sunshine's belly, his right arm between the Indian's legs, and straightened up. He slowly turned on the log that was support-ing them, moved down its length toward shore, jumped to another log, walked the length of that one, then stepped on top of several logs running lengthwise of the river until he finally stepped down into the shallow water near shore.

On reading this passage, it may well have occurred to you that it takes Eammon an awful long time to make it to shore. The Indian, Sunshine, has been hurt and the reader doesn't yet know how badly hurt, and there's a great deal of action both before and after this point—the scene is an exciting one. But the author undermines the excitement by his blow-by-blow (or log-by-log) account of how Eammon made his way to land. The time spent on a relatively minor point has thrown the scene out of proportion.

Proportion problems like this one probably arise for the same reason as do problems with repetition—it's hard to judge the effect your writing will have on your readers while you are writing it, so you tend to go overboard. While writing the passage quoted above, the author presumably felt it was vital that his readers picture Eammon's journey over the logs precisely as he himself saw it.

And this sort of proportion problem has exactly the same effect on readers as does repetition. When you fill in all the details and leave nothing to your readers' imaginations, you are patronizing them. This is even more true now than it was a few decades ago, when generous, detailed descriptions were the norm. It's the influence of movies and television again—readers are used to quick jump-cuts from scene to scene rather than long transitional shots. Fiction writers, in turn, are much more free to use ellipses, to leave more of the mundane, bridging action up to their readers' imaginations.

For instance, instead of writing:

> The phone rang. Geraldine walked across the room and picked it up. "Hello," she said.

An author nowadays can simply write

> The phone rang.
> "Hello," Geraldine said.

and leave the rest of the action to the reader's imagination. And the author of the example at the beginning of this chapter needed only to write:

> Eammon flung the peavey to shore, grabbed Sunshine by his jacket collar and belt, threw him over his shoulder, and made his way across the logs to shore.

Of course, the proportions of your writing can go off in other ways besides descriptive detail. In Chapter 1, we talked at length about balancing the narrative summary/immediate scenes proportion in favor of scenes. And in Chapter 2, we warned against spending too much time on flashbacks to your characters' pasts.

There's another good reason to be wary of flashbacks. Even when they don't make your plot difficult to follow, flashbacks can rob your story of its drive. When events unfold from beginning to end, they start to pick up a momentum that, properly handled, can make your conclusion seem inevitable. But once you start to play with the timeline, you're likely to introduce a sense of aimlessness into your story. Of course, sometimes a flashback is the only way to develop your plot, and some authors write flashbacks so powerfully and well that they achieve power and momentum within themselves. But the best approach is to violate chronology only when you have an excellent reason for doing so. Spend the largest proportion of your time in the present.

Some years ago, we worked on a first novel whose author had used a great many well-written flashbacks to show her readers how her heroine got to be the way she is. The novel was rejected by several publishers, one of whose editors said she "would have bought it if there were no flashbacks." The author put the novel through a final draft, eliminating virtually all of the flashbacks, and it was signed up by the next publisher to see it. Both drafts were skillfully written, both were suspenseful. But eliminating the flashbacks gave the final draft a quality of inexorability that made it riveting.

Sometimes proportion problems arise when an author is writing about his or her pet interests or hobbies. We once worked on a thriller that involved a seventeen-year-old boy making his way across the country, living off the land as he went. The book was generally well written, and the author—evidently something of a survivalist himself—was given to precise, detailed descriptions of survival techniques, such as the best way to lash yourself to a tree limb so you won't fall off while you sleep.

Admittedly these details created an atmosphere of authenticity and established the author's authority as a survivalist. And, yes, one of the joys of reading comes about when an author takes you through some little back alley of life that you never knew existed. But when we reached the three pages on how to kill and field-dress a beaver, we decided the author had gone too far.

Even in the nineteenth century, the age of the long attention span, Melville created a lot of problems for readers of *Moby Dick* by including lengthy passages on the natural history of whales. After all, it's easy to drop out of a work of fiction that has pages and pages of passages like the following:

> BOOK II. (Octavo), CHAPTER I. (Grampus).—Though this fish, whose loud sonorous breathing, or rather blowing, has furnished a proverb to landsmen, is so well known a denizen of the deep, yet is he not popularly classed among whales. But possessing all the grand distinctive features of the leviathan, most naturalists have recognized him for one. He is of moderate octavo size, varying from fifteen to twenty-five feet in length, and is usually most stylishly dressed. He swims in herds, and has been seen in habitats as varied as the grand salons of the lower east side and the alehouses of Canarsie. Although an accomplished dancer, the Grampus is widely known as a poor conversationalist, and therefore should be avoided in most social situations . . .

You didn't read the whole paragraph, did you? If so, you are not alone. The chapter on Cetology in *Moby Dick* may well be the least-read chapter in great American literature.

In a more recent example, Tom Clancy has drawn barbs on the proportion front, as in this excerpt from an otherwise favorable review by Morton Kondracke in *The New York Times Book Review*:

> As in all his previous novels, this one bulges with technological verisimilitude. In the earlier books, Mr. Clancy taught his readers more than any but experts could possibly absorb about

"Right about now the editors have reached the three pages on how to kill and field dress a beaver...."

submarine operations; air, land and sea war strategy; satellite photography; ballistic missiles and missile defense; small unit tactics, and the highest of high-tech communications. In this novel, he does the same with nuclear bomb fabrication, though he says in a postscript that he has altered some details so no one could use the novel to build a bomb.

In its plotting, vividness and suspense, this is Mr. Clancy's best book since *The Hunt for Red October*. To sustain interest, however, we simply do not have to watch each turn of the lathe and each shaving of plutonium that goes into making an H-bomb. This book remains a whiz-bang page-turner, but to be honest, not all the pages get read.

Proportion problems can also arise inadvertently, through cutting. That's what happened to one of our editors, Judith Searle, whose first novel, *Lovelife*, was put under contract at seven hundred pages during the era when the editor who signed up a book actually edited the manuscripts. Judith's editor made a number of suggestions for cuts: philosophical passages, cooking scenes, passages of interior monologue . . . .

Soon the manuscript was trimmed to size. Gone were nearly all the cooking scenes, most of the philosophical and descriptive passages, and a fair amount of the interior monologue. Left intact were all the sex scenes. The result was a very steamy novel indeed, since the cuts radically changed the proportion of sex scenes to the novel as a whole.

However your proportion problems may arise, the most serious effect they can have on your writing is to mislead the reader. When you spend a great deal of time on one character or plot element for whatever reason, your readers naturally assume that element to be important. So if the character you spend time on turns out to be insignificant or the plot element you set up in such detail never comes into play, readers are going to feel cheated.

In the first draft of a science fiction novel we edited, the author devoted many pages to the nature of American society a century from now—developing, along the way, some penetrating insights into society as it is today. But after spending the first half of the book on this future society, the author resolved the plot without involving that society at all. Instead, his hero simply resolved some personal problems and then went on to live happily ever after. Since we expected him to use the society he'd created in such detail, we felt cheated by the ending, as if the book ended before it was over. In the next draft the author gave more emphasis to his character's personal problems earlier in the book and also involved the futuristic society in his ending. The result was a much more satisfying story.

How do you go about spotting and solving proportion problems? The best way is to approach your work as if you were reading it for the first time. This isn't easy to do, of course—

which is why editors come in so handy—but you may gain enough objectivity to do it if you walk away from your writing for a few days or weeks.

When you come back, print out a scene or chapter and read it over. (You'll get better results if you read hard copy rather than disk.) The idea is to react to the scene like a reader, not a writer. As you read, ask yourself what interests you the most, what really comes to life, what involves and intrigues. What moves or fascinates or disturbs or pleases you? Note your reactions in the margins or on post-it slips. Don't analyze your reactions—this is not an intellectual exercise. And don't make any changes. Yet.

Once you've figured out what you like, take a look at what's left: Is it really needed? Does it add? (It may not be *needed*, yet add nonetheless.) Should it be shorter? Longer? This simple process can be surprisingly effective, because what interests you the most is, very often, what's going to be of the most interest to your readers. If you feel uncomfortable with the length of a passage, the amount of detail, or the number of observations made by a character, then your reader's reaction is likely to be at least as negative as yours.

The technique may not work when your proportions are off, because you're writing about your pet interests. After all, writing and reading about your favorite activity can be a lot of fun, so it's hard to tell how much is too much. And when you're writing about something you know well and love dearly, you are usually writing at your best.

But again, putting some distance between yourself and your manuscript can help you recognize when you're lending your story authenticity and when you're belaboring your favorite topic or showing off your research. And if you're describing something you feel passionate about, whether it's eighteenth-century theosophy, hand-cranking homemade ice cream, or the varieties of wildflower in a Blue Ridge mountain meadow, bear in mind that your readers may not find these topics nearly as interesting as you do.

The next step is to try cutting (or reworking) those passages that upon rereading no longer seem to belong in the scene. Be forewarned: don't ruthlessly delete everything that doesn't advance your plot. That would result in a novel with no texture. All we're suggesting is that you attribute to your readers the same responsive capability you yourself possess. If instead of patronizing your readers you assume them to be intelligent and perceptive, they're likely to return the compliment.

And once you train yourself to see how changes in proportion affect your writing, you can begin to use proportion to shape your reader's response to your plot. If you have some plot development that you want to come as a surprise, spend less space on it before you spring it on your readers. Or perhaps you could spend as much or more space on similar plot elements to mask the really important one.

Agatha Christie used this technique in her first Miss Marple novel, *Murder at the Vicarage*. In that novel, Miss Marple was not yet known as a shrewd detective—she was simply one more doddering old woman in a village amply supplied with doddering old women. So it came as that much more of a surprise when she gently explained exactly how the murder was committed and by whom. Had Christie devoted pages to Miss Marple's deductive powers, the effect would have been lost.

An early draft of Fran Dorf's remarkable second novel, *Flight*, presented the author with a proportion challenge. Two of the main characters in *Flight* are Alan, the son of the town doctor, and Ethan, the son of the local crazy lady. Ethan, convicted of pushing his girlfriend Lana off a cliff, has been out of prison for eight years. Eventually the reader learns that it wasn't crazy Ethan who pushed Lana off the cliff, it was Alan; and through most of the book Ethan and Lana lead Alan's brother through a discovery of the truth.

The proportion problem arose because it was important to develop Alan's character in considerable detail. He was her villain, and the plot pivoted on an understanding of his personality. But because she spent so much time on Alan, her readers were likely to assume that Alan must be up to something—and so to guess early on that he was the culprit.

The author solved this problem by having Ethan escape from prison at the beginning of the novel rather than being released eight years earlier. She also added scenes in which an unidentified character (Ethan, of course) stalked Alan—which set up Alan as a potential victim and so gave the author a logical reason to develop his character. In effect, she controlled the proportions of her plot in order to mislead her readers.

As you come to understand how proportion affects the way your readers see your story, you'll not only be able to correct the proportion when it's out of whack, you'll also be able to use proportion to control your readers' response to your work. The technique is subtle but powerful, for it enables you to manipulate your readers without their knowing they are being manipulated.

When *Devices and Desires* appeared, P. D. James's publisher had another bestseller, her fans another powerful, satisfying reading experience, and reviewers another chance to point out that James is a superb novelist who just happens to write murder mysteries. But in this particular novel the proportion of in-depth, detailed characterization and description to murder and detection had many readers and some reviewers grumbling.

A look at the beginning of Chapter Three suggests why:

Dalgleish had spent Sunday morning revisiting Norwich Cathedral and St. Peter Mancroft before lunching at a restaurant on the outskirts of the city where he and his aunt two years previously had eaten an unpretentious but excellently cooked meal. But here too time had wrought its changes . . . [There follows a precise description of decor and meal.]

During the last four years it had been rare for him to visit his aunt without driving with her to Salle, and she had left with her will a request that her ashes be strewn in the churchyard there without ceremony and by him on his own. [There follow Dalgleish's thoughts about the oddity of this request, his aunt's unreligious nature, his own sense of "a duty to perform" and theories about man's "insistent need for ritual."]

He turned off the B1149 at Felthorpe to take the country

roads across the flat country. It was unnecessary to consult the map. The magnificent fifteenth-century tower with its four pinnacles was an unmistakable landmark, and he drove towards it along the almost deserted roads with the familiar sense of coming home. [There follow his thoughts about the beloved aunt whose ashes he is carrying, his impression of the church and churchyard, a moment of quiet in which he absorbs his surroundings, his relief that no priest is on hand to necessitate explanations or complications, and, finally, his scattering of the ashes to a verse recalled from Ecclesiastes.]

For three more pages we accompany Dalgleish on his personal rounds, enjoying (or growing impatient with) his contemplative turn of mind and James's leisurely way of conveying it as he takes a walk. Until:

> He switched on his torch and played it over the path. It caught the gleam of something white to his left, a sheet of newspaper, perhaps, a handkerchief, a discarded paper bag. Feeling no more than mild curiosity, he stepped from the path to investigate. And then he saw her. . . .[There follows a detailed, sharply conceived and executed discovery of a body, complete with Dalgleish's brilliantly conveyed emotional reactions to the discovery.]

Even those of James's fans (and reviewers) who are impatient with her tours of the English countryside and Adam Dalgleish's mind will trust her to deliver the goods, mystery-wise. But there *are*, arguably, grounds for considering some of the leisurely passages in *Devices and Desires* disproportionately long.

That might seem to be the case with James's previous mystery, *A Taste for Death*, in which we spend all of Chapter Seven in the apartment of Dalgleish's assistant, Kate Miskin. She looks around the rooms, giving some thought to her interior and exterior landscape, then switches on her answering machine:

. . . And with the first sound of the familiar voice, euphoria died to be replaced by a confusion of guilt, resentment, and depression. It was her grandmother's social worker. There were three messages, at two-hour intervals, controlled professional patience gradually giving way to frustration and, finally, an irritation that was close to hostility. Her grandmother, weary of incarceration in her seventh-floor flat, had gone out to the post office to collect her pension and had come back to find that the window had been smashed and an attempt made to force the door. It was the third such incident in less than a month. Mrs. Miskin was now too apprehensive to go out. Would Kate please ring the local authority social services department as soon as she got in, or, if it was after five-thirty, ring her grandmother direct? It was urgent.

Why, a reader might reasonably wonder, are we spending so much time with the assistant detective's sense of obligation to the grandmother who raised her? But in this case the author's sense of proportion is dead-on. Kate ends up reluctantly sacrificing her privacy to give sanctuary to her grandmother—who holds center stage two hundred pages later in the exciting and profoundly disturbing denouement whose effect on the reader would be much less profound had we not come to know (and care about) Kate Miskin and her domestic situation.

So when you're self-editing for proportion, don't be too quick to decide that a tangent belongs on the cutting room floor. Read with the sharpest possible awareness of your own response as a reader—and your author's knowledge of where a side trip is leading two hundred pages down the road—and you're likely to make the right decisions about balancing your story elements.

CHECKLIST
• How much of your time have you spent moving your characters around? Do you cut from location to location, or do you fill in all the space in between?

• How much detail have you included in describing your character's actions? Try cutting some of the detail and see if the actions are still clear.

• Are you writing about your favorite topics or hobbies? If so, give careful consideration to how much time you spend on them.

• Take a look at your flashbacks. How often are you interrupting the forward flow of your story? Do you have flashbacks at more than one level—that is, flashbacks from flashbacks? If you spend nearly as much time in the past as in the present, take a look at each flashback individually. If it were cut, would the present story be harder to follow?

• How much space do you devote to each of your main characters? Is the amount of space justified by their place in the plot?

• Do you have tangents—little subplots or descriptions that don't directly advance the plot? If so, are all of them effective? If not, should you add some?

EXERCISES
A. *Correct the proportion in the following:*

As he approached the last hill, Carter passed two more runners who had started fast but were now spent and fading. They could no longer keep their arms up; their stride, once crisp and high-stepping, was now a tired, struggling, agonized shuffle. They licked their lips; their heads and shoulders drooped and swung desperately from side to side as if that extra motion could somehow coax additional reserve and speed from their aching legs.

CHAPTER 11

SOPHISTICATION

As she walked toward the kitchen, Heather peeled off various items of clothing. The image she projected of neatness, she thought, was just that—an image. Heather was a slob at heart.

Stopping in the entranceway to the kitchen, she leaned against the door frame and peeled off her panty hose. As she tossed them toward the top of the refrigerator, she breathed a sigh of relief. She was still hot, but at least she was free of the confines of clothing. Now for something to eat, she thought as she stood in front of the refrigerator.

You're likely to have spotted a couple of self-editing problems (such as the repetitions and speaker attributions with interior monologue) in the above passage. And correcting for the self-editing points we have covered so far will help make any writing seem more professional. But you can also easily learn a few stylistic tricks that will give your writing that extra bit of sophistication. These tricks range from avoiding legitimate constructions that have been overused by hack writers to finding alternatives to certain stylistic techniques that have virtually disappeared over the last few decades. But whatever it is that makes these mechanics sophisticated, awareness of them when revising will help your work look like that of a professional rather than an amateur.

One easy way to make your writing seem more sophisticated is to avoid two stylistic constructions that are common to hack writers, namely:

Pulling off her gloves, she turned to face him.

or

As she pulled off her gloves, she turned to face him.

Both the *as* construction and the *-ing* construction as used above are grammatically correct and express the action clearly and unambiguously. But notice that both of these constructions take a bit of action ("She pulled off her gloves") and tuck it away into a dependent clause ("Pulling off her gloves . . ."). This tends to place some of your action at one remove from your reader, to make the actions seem incidental, unimportant. And so if you use these constructions often, you weaken your writing.

Another reason to avoid the *as* and *-ing* constructions is that they sometimes give rise to physical impossibilities. We once worked on the autobiography of a behavioral biologist who, in the process of describing her field work, wrote, "Disappearing into my tent, I changed into fresh jeans." The *-ing* construction forces simultaneity on two actions that can't be simultaneous. The doctor didn't duck into the tent and pull on clean pants at the same time—she was a biologist, not a contortionist.

We're not suggesting that you avoid these phrases altogether. There are going to be times when you want to write about two actions that are actually simultaneous, or when an action is genuinely incidental and deserves no more than a dependent clause. And given the choice between an *as* or *-ing* construction and a belabored, artificial alternative, you're well advised to use the *as* or *-ing*. But do avoid the hack's favorite constructions unless you have a good reason for using them.

Learn to spot these constructions and, if you see more than one or two on a page, start hunting around for alternatives. For instance, "Pulling off her gloves, she turned to face him" could easily be changed to "She pulled off her gloves and turned to face him," or even "She pulled off her gloves, turned to face him." Or you can make an *-ing* phrase less conspicuous by moving it to the middle of the sentence rather than the beginning. The participle construction has a particularly amateurish flavor when placed at the beginning of a sentence.

To see just how much these constructions can weaken your writing, take a look at the rest of the scene we quoted at the beginning of the chapter, with the *as* and *-ing* constructions in boldfaced type:

> **Ripping off several large, dripping hunks of burrito**, she pulled up a chair to the kitchen table and took a large bite. **As she chewed**, she wondered who she was maddest at. Clark, she decided.
>
> The doorbell rang. "Heather, it's me!" boomed a deep, authoritative voice. "Clark!"
>
> **Spotting her favorite red silk kimono crumpled on the floor**, Heather stooped over and picked it up. **As she pulled the kimono over her shoulders**, she said a prayer of thanks that the wrinkled look was in.
>
> **As her fingers unfastened the chain lock**, she wondered how Clark had gotten her address. It wasn't listed in the telephone book.
>
> "Good evening," Clark greeted with a small bow **as the door swung open**.
>
> "The bug man came last week," Heather said sarcastically, **refusing to budge from the door**. "I thought he'd exterminated all the pests in my life, but I guess he must have missed one. A big one."
>
> "Funny, very funny," Clark said, clearly not amused **as he**

leaned an arm against the door jamb. "Now you'd better let me in before I start causing a scene."

Now take a look at the same scene again, with the *as* and *-ing* clauses removed, along with some of the other self-editing problems:

> She pulled up a chair to the kitchen table and took a large bite of the burrito she'd found behind the milk and orange juice bottles. Who was she maddest at? Probably Clark.
>
> The doorbell rang. "Heather, it's me!"
>
> *Clark.* It had to be.
>
> Heather sighed, stooped over and picked up her red silk kimono from the floor. Thank god the wrinkled look was in. But how had Clark gotten her address? It wasn't listed in the telephone book.
>
> "Good evening." He made a small bow.
>
> "The bug man came last week." Heather didn't budge from the door. "I thought he'd exterminated all the pests in my life, but I guess he must have missed a big one."
>
> "Funny, very funny," Clark leaned an arm against the door jamb. "You'd better let me in before I start causing a scene."

Admittedly this still isn't deathless prose, but the editing *has* made the passage subtler and more professional.

Another way to keep from looking like an amateur is to avoid the use of clichés. Virtually all clichés, of course, begin their life as original, effective expressions—so effective, in fact, that they are used until all the life goes out of them. So if you come across lifeless passages, you may need to self-edit for the purpose of weeding out any clichés. Your characters should never live life in the fast lane, nor should anything in your writing be worth no more than a plugged nickel. And if you come across "She tossed her head," the first question you should ask is, "How far?"

Watch for clichés on the larger scale, too, particularly in the creation of minor characters. Don't outfit your accountants in

coke-bottle glasses and pocket protectors, or make your clergy-
men mild and soft-spoken, or let your New York cabbies drive
like maniacs (although, arguably, this last example is nothing
more than simple accuracy). When you fall into characterization clichés like these, the result is a cartoon rather than a
character.

One caveat: in narration, there may be times when you need
to use a familiar, pet phrase—yes, a cliché—to summarize a
complicated situation. But before going with the cliché, give
some thought to the possibility of "turning" it, altering it
slightly to render the phrasing less familiar. In a celebrated
novel we edited, the author used the phrase "they vanished
into thin air" to avoid a lengthy, complicated explanation. We
suggested a change to "they vanished into thick air," which fit
the poetic, steamy atmosphere of the European city in which
the scene was set.

In Chapter 4, we warned you to watch out for -*ly* adverbs
when you're writing dialogue. But even when you're not writing dialogue, be on the lookout for -*ly* adverbs, for the sake of
sophistication. Chances are, as you bang out your first draft,
you use the first verbs that come to mind—verbs that are com-
monplace and comfortable, verbs you don't have to dig too
deep to find. "Set," for instance, as in:

"She set the cup and saucer on the kitchen table."

Then, since "set" doesn't really convey what you want, you
find the extra nuance you need in an adjective, tack on an -*ly* to
make an adverb, and stick it to the verb.

"Angrily she set the cup and saucer on the kitchen table."

This approach may be all right for a first draft, but when you
self-edit, you can root out these verb/adverb combinations like
the weeds they are. The weak verbs that came to mind so readily
can then be jettisoned in favor of stronger, more specific verbs—
verbs that can say exactly what you want to say without help.

"She slammed the cup and saucer onto the kitchen table."

When you use two words (a weak verb and an adverb) to do the work of one (a strong verb) you dilute your writing and rob it of its potential power.

There are exceptions, of course, as there are to every principle in this book. If your heroine has just finished the restoration of her 1952 MG-TD, a project she has been working on for the last nine years, you might be compelled to write:

"She tightened the last nut—slowly, lovingly."

It's not terrific writing but it's an understandable solution—there probably isn't a single verb in the English language that can convey this particular way of tightening a nut. But even where the adverbs aren't the product of lazy writing, they can still *look* like lazy writing, just because -*ly* adverbs have been used so often by so many hacks in the past. It might be better to rewrite the description of the car from your heroine's point of view and in her voice so that we can see she loves it, without your having to say so. To show us rather than tell us.

A simple departure from conventional comma usage can also lend a modern, sophisticated touch to your fiction—especially your dialogue. All you have to do is string together short sentences with commas instead of separating them with periods, as in these examples:

"I tried to tell him, I couldn't get his attention."
"Hurry up, let's get going."
"Don't worry about it, she's only sixteen."

This comma usage, if not overdone, conveys remarkably well the way speech actually falls on the ear. Most of us don't come to a full stop after every sentence when we're talking, nor do your characters have to. And this special effect needn't be reserved exclusively for dialogue passages. In *Billy Bathgate*, E. L. Doctorow often comma-strings sentences of narration:

[He said] "Hey, young fellow, what's the younger generation reading these days?" as if it was really important to him. He turned the book up in my hand so he could read the title, I don't know what he had expected, a French novel maybe, but he was genuinely surprised.

There are a few stylistic devices that are so "tacky" they should be used *very* sparingly, if at all. First on the list is emphasis quotes—as in the quotes around the word "tacky" in the preceding sentence. The only time you need use them is to show you are referring to the word itself, as we do in the second sentence in this paragraph. Read it again; it all makes sense.

Then there are the stylistic devices that make a writer look insecure, the most notable offenders being exclamation points and italics. Exclamation points should be reserved for moments when a character is physically shouting (or experiencing the mental equivalent). When you use them frequently, you begin to look as if you are trying desperately to infuse your dialogue or narration with an excitement it lacks. And frequent italics are the typographical equivalent of an elbow in the ribs and a frantic, "Did you get it? Did you?"

Articles and short stories in *Cosmopolitan* magazine make such frequent use of italics and exclamation points that the result is a gushy, girlish, hyped-up style easy to parody:

"Oh, *God*!" Samantha said, "do you know what he *did*? He picked me up and *threw* me onto the bed, and then he just *flung* himself on *top of me*! I tell you, Shirley, I was in seventh *heaven*!"

Should you need any further convincing on this point, note what happens to a poignant confrontation between mother and daughter in Mary Gordon's *The Company of Women* when you hype it up with just a few exclamation points and italics:

"I should *never* have let you go up there to Columbia. I should have known they'd take advantage of you!"

"Nobody took advantage of me, Mother."

"Then how did you get in *this* condition?" she said through her teeth.

"I got into this condition because I used the wrong kind of birth control!"

"Don't talk about that in this house!"

I had forgotten: in my mother's canon, practicing birth control was worse than having sex.

"Whose is it?" she asked. "That goddamn professor, right?"

"I'm not sure."

"Don't try and protect him. I *know* you."

"I'm not sure whose it is, Mother. I slept with two people. I'm not sure which one is the father!"

"Fine," said my mother. "Very nice. Just *beautiful!*"

That was the last she has ever spoken about the father of my child. There was not a *word* of forced marriages, not a mention of paternity suits. Which is remarkable, since she is, if nothing else, a woman who believes in convention.

Now read the passage as the author wrote it:

"I should never have let you go up there to Columbia. I should have known they'd take advantage of you."

"Nobody took advantage of me, Mother."

"Then how did you get in this condition?" she said through her teeth.

"I got into this condition because I used the wrong kind of birth control."

"Don't talk about that in this house."

I had forgotten: in my mother's canon, practicing birth control was worse than having sex.

"Whose is it?" she asked. "That goddamn professor, right?"

"I'm not sure."

"Don't try and protect him. I know you."

"I'm not sure whose it is, Mother. I slept with two people. I'm not sure which one is the father."

"Fine," said my mother. "Very nice. Just beautiful."

That was the last she has ever spoken about the father of my child. There was not a word of forced marriages, not a mention of paternity suits. Which is remarkable, since she is, if nothing else, a woman who believes in convention.

You can see that the dialogue and description convey all the emotion needed. And the author's voice, without the lexical trappings, is calm and confident.

There's another stylistic device whose overuse will brand you as an amateur: flowery, poetic figures of speech, much beloved by beginning writers and used very sparingly by the pros. If you're a poet, and most of your imagery is fresh and strong, reining yourself in may be more difficult than you might think. Take a look at this excerpt from Peter Cooper's novel *Billy Shakes*, in which a character has just learned that his wife is pregnant:

> "The trouble with women," Hoot said with a serious smile, "is that they always seem to think they have everything figured out. When the truth is, they don't know a thing."
>
> "Come on, Hoot," Lucy said. "Admit it. You're a father."
>
> "As a matter of fact, Lucy, it may be that Rose is pregnant." His eyes were a dark, dark blue, stolen jewels in a setting of bone. "But I can assure you that I am not the father."
>
> "What are you saying?" she asked in a horrified whisper.
>
> "I *can't* have children. That's what I'm saying." He paused to light a cigarette, his hand shaking ever so slightly. "It just so happens that I had a vasectomy a year before I married Rose."

The metaphor, the dark blue stolen jewels in a setting of bone, isn't bad, although it's weak in comparison to some of the ones this fine poet has been known to invoke. Yet the problem isn't the unworkability of the metaphor but its presence in the scene in the first place. This scene is the moment on which the plot of the entire novel turns—we find out in the next few paragraphs that Hoot's best friend, Lucy's husband, is the father of Rose's child. Yet just when it's most important that we focus on events, we're pulled aside to notice the author's poetic gift. This doesn't happen in the edited version:

> "The trouble with women," Hoot said with a serious smile, "is that they always seem to think they have everything figured out. When the truth is, they don't know a thing."
>
> "Come on, Hoot," Lucy said. "Admit it. You're a father."
>
> His eyes were a dark, dark blue. "As a matter of fact, Lucy, it may be that Rose is pregnant. But I can assure you that I am not the father."
>
> "What are you saying?"
>
> "I *can't* have children. That's what I'm saying." He paused to light a cigarette, his hand shaking ever so slightly. "It just so happens that I had a vasectomy a year before I married Rose."

Note that in the edited version a dialogue explanation ("she asked in a horrified whisper") has been cut along with the metaphor, since the emotional quality of the scene in context makes Lucy's dialogue more than adequate to convey her horror. As for the metaphor, its absence keeps the reader's focus where the author wants it—on the confrontation/revelation, not the figure of speech. Like exclamation points or italics, phrases that call attention to themselves rather than to what's being said will make it obvious that you're working hard for your effects.

When it comes to handling sex scenes, the last thing you want is to seem to be working hard to achieve your effects. The subtler stylistic approach will nearly always be the more professional-looking choice. This means you'll want to avoid heavy breathing, whether it's the type appropriate to novels with titles like *Love's Helpless Fury* or the type common to novels with titles like *Motel Lust* or *Lust Motel*. There was a time when explicit sex scenes added a sense of sophistication, of authenticity to a book (to say nothing of boosting sales). But in a day when photographs that once would have been sold under the counter are used to advertise blue jeans, this approach has lost its power to shock or titillate.

The subtle approach, on the other hand, engages your reader's imagination and so is likely to be far more effective. This is an area where it might be a good idea to bring back an old-fashioned narrative convention: sexual encounters that take place in linespaces. After all, if you leave the physical details to your readers' imaginations, they are likely to be far more engaged than if you spell it all out. A line space may be a far more erotic place for two charcters to make love than a bed.

For instance, take a look at what is arguably the most famous sex scene in modern literature, from Margaret Mitchell's *Gone With the Wind*:

He swung her off her feet and into his arms and started up the stairs. Her head was crushed against his chest and she heard the hard hammering of his heart beneath her ears. He hurt her and she cried out, muffled, frightened. Up the stairs he went in the utter darkness, up, up, and she was wild with fear. He was a mad stranger and this was a black darkness she did not know, darker than death. He was like death, carrying her away in arms that hurt. She screamed, stifled against him and he stopped suddenly on the landing and, turning her swiftly in his arms, bent over her and kissed her with a savagery and completeness that wiped out everything from her mind but the dark into which she was sinking and the lips on hers. He was shaking, as though he stood in a strong wind, and his lips, fallen from her body, fell on her soft flesh. He was muttering things she did not hear, his lips were evoking feelings never felt before. She was darkness and he was darkness and there had never been anything before this time, only darkness and his lips on hers. She tried to speak and his mouth was over her again. Suddenly she had a wild thrill such as she had never known; joy, fear, madness, excitement, surrender to arms that were too strong, lips too bruising, fate that moved too fast. For the first time in her life she had met someone, something stronger than she, someone she could neither bully nor break, someone who was bullying and breaking her. Somehow, her arms were around his neck and her lips trembling beneath his and they were going up, up

"Since now profanity and explicit sex scenes are no longer in vogue Maynard feels all his years of education and preparation were for naught."

into the darkness again, a darkness that was soft and swirling and all enveloping.

When she awoke the next morning, he was gone and had it not been for the rumpled pillow beside her, she would have thought the happenings of the night before a preposterous dream . . . .

A modern editor might break this up into another paragraph or two—we certainly would. But no editor in his/her right mind would add explicit sexual or anatomical details. The effectiveness of the scene in evoking the reader's imagination is as much in force today as it was in the late 1930s.

And what is true of sexual details is also true of profanity. There was a time when your characters were worldly and streetwise if they swore a lot. But profanity has been so overused in past years that nowadays it's just a sign of a small vocabulary. Of course, if profanity is appropriate to your character, then have your character swear. But if you include a lot of profanity for the sake of sophistication or shock value, it's likely to do nothing more than turn your readers off. And think about how much power a single expletive can have if it's the only one in the whole fucking book.

The surest sign that you are achieving literary sophistication is when your writing begins to seem effortless. Not that it will *be* effortless, of course—crafting good prose is hard work. We often work with authors through four drafts before we see the novel published, although the first draft we see may not be the first one the author wrote.

And the goal of all this careful, conscious work is to produce a novel or short story collection that reads as though no hard labor were involved in producing it. Fred Astaire worked tirelessly to make dancing look like the easiest, most natural thing in the world. And that's what you're trying for—a level of effectiveness that can make what was hardest to achieve look easy.

CHECKLIST

• How many *-ing* and *-as* phrases do you write? It may be time to get out the highlighters and mark them all. Remember, the only ones that count are the ones that place a bit of action in a subordinate clause.

• How about *-ly* adverbs? Both tied to your dialogue and within your descriptions and narration.

• Do you have a lot of short sentences, both within your dialogue and within your description and narration? Try stringing some of them together with commas.

• Do you use a lot of italics? We mean a *lot* of italics? And you don't use many exclamation points, do you?!

• Are there any metaphors or flowery phrases you're particularly proud of? Do they come at key times during your plot? If so, think about getting rid of them.

• How much of your sex scenes do you leave to your readers' imaginations?

• Are you using a lot of profanity?

EXERCISES
A. *Edit this paragraph, taken from Kathleen E. Woodiwiss's* The Wolf and the Dove, *for sophistication (romance writers take note: Woodiwiss is a bestselling author despite—not because of—her style):*

Grabbing up a pelt she pulled it close about her and gave him a impishly wicked look as she grinned. Turning on her heels with a low laugh, she went to the hearth, there to lay small logs upon the still warm coals. She blew upon them but drew back in haste as the ashes flew up and sat back upon her heels rubbing her reddened eyes while Wulfgar's amused chuckles filled the room. She made a face at his mirth and swung the kettle of water on its hook over the building heat as he crossed to the warmth of the fire beside her and began to dress.

B. A little historical editing. The conventions Lewis Carroll used in Alice in Wonderland *were perfectly acceptable when he wrote it and don't really interfere with the genius of the book. But still they are clunky and cumbersome by today's standards. So try your hand at the following passage.*

All this time Tweedledee was trying his best to fold up the umbrella, with himself in it, which was such an extraordinary thing to do that it quite took off Alice's attention from the angry brother. But he couldn't quite succeed, and it ended in his rolling over, bundled up in the umbrella, with only his head out; and there he lay, opening and shutting his mouth and his large eyes—"looking more like a fish than anything else," Alice thought.

"Of course you agree to have a battle?" Tweedledum said in a calmer tone.

"I suppose so," the other sulkily replied, as he crawled out of the umbrella; "only *she* must help us dress up, you know."

So the two brothers went off hand in hand into the wood, and returned, in a minute, with their arms full of things—such as bolsters, blankets, hearthrugs, tablecloths, dish covers, and coal scuttles. "I hope you're a good hand at pinning and tying strings?" Tweedledum remarked. "Every one of these things has got to go on, somehow or other."

Alice said afterward she had never seen such a fuss made about anything in all her life—the way those two bustled about, and the quantity of things they put on, and the trouble they gave her in tying strings and fastening buttons—"Really, they'll be more like bundles of old clothes than anything else by the time they're ready!" she said to herself, as she arranged a bolster round the neck of Tweedledee, "to keep his head from being cut off," as he said.

"You know," he added very gravely, "it's one of the most serious things that can possibly happen to one in a battle, to get one's head cut off."

C. The Final Exercise. This was written by one of the authors as an workshop exercise. Be warned: every self-editing point we've mentioned in the book so far can be found in this one exercise.

"But Ernestine, honey," Winthrop breathed, "I swear I was never anywhere near the John Smith motel!"

"Winthrop, *darling*," Ernestine said sarcastically, "that's not what I heard from Helena." She looked out the window.

Winthrop found himself looking at his hands. He scuffed the carpet with his foot, feeling like a small boy with a baseball bat in front of a broken window. But then his gorge began to rise at the injustice of it. "No!" he thought, defiant, "I intend to brazen it out." Helena Basquette was known to be the trouble-making type.

"Ernestine," he said sincerely. "You should have better sense than to trust to the ramblings of as big a fool as Helena Basquette. Why only last week ..."

The doorbell rang resoundingly.

Laying her cigar carefully on the ashtray at her arm, Ernestine crossed the room and opened the door.

The young man silhouetted against the streetlight was tall, his shock of black hair glimmering faintly with condensation from the evening fog. Over his lanky frame he wore a loose-fitting bomber jacket and faded, stone-washed jeans.

And in his hand, that familiar square box.

"You the guys what ordered the pizza?" he snarled.

Ernestine looked away. "Winthrop, *sweetie*," she continued bitingly, "are you responsible for this outrage?"

"Oh, no," thought the pizza man. "He's been fightin' wid his old lady. I ain't gonna get no tip outta this one."

CHAPTER 12

VOICE

An early seafaring novel by a celebrated nineteenth-century novelist begins with this paragraph:

> It was the middle of a bright tropical afternoon that we made good our escape from the bay. The vessel we sought lay with her main-topsail aback about a league from the land and was the only object that broke the broad expanse of the ocean.

Years later the novelist wrote another first-person seafaring novel that begins:

> Call me Ishmael. Some years ago—never mind how long precisely—having little or no money in my purse, and nothing particular to interest me on shore, I thought I would sail about a little and see the watery part of the world . . .

The opening of *Omoo* is slightly intriguing and gives a clear and vivid picture of the waiting ship. The opening of

Moby Dick is irresistible. What makes the difference?

The answer, of course, is voice. And judging by the writing style in these two Herman Melville novels, even the greatest voices develop over time. Certainly at the time when he wrote *Omoo*, Melville had not yet found what John Gardner (in *On Becoming a Novelist*) has called "his booming, authoritative voice." In the *Moby Dick* opening, Gardner points out, the rhythms "lift and roll, pause, gather, roll again." The authority is unmistakable.

Of course, the writer's voice in a novel generally belongs to a character. The voice in *Moby Dick* belongs to Ishmael as much as it does to Melville. But character voice and authorial voice are intimately connected, as you can see in the passages that follow in which we meet the protagonist in each novel:

> I am doomed to remember a boy with a wrecked voice—not because of his voice, or because he was the smallest person I ever knew, or even because he was the instrument of my mother's death, but because he is the reason I believe in God; I am a Christian because of Owen Meany.
> —JOHN IRVING, *A Prayer for Owen Meany*

> I have just returned from a visit to my landlord—the solitary neighbor that I shall be troubled with. This is certainly a beautiful country! In all England, I do not believe that I could have fixed on a situation so completely removed from the stir of society. A perfect misanthropist's heaven; and Mr. Heathcliff and I are such a suitable pair to divide the desolation between us.
> —EMILY BRONTE, *Wuthering Heights*

> Somebody asked in English: "What did you say?"
> Mr. Tench swivelled round. "You English?" he said in astonishment, but at the sight of the round and hollow face charred with a three days' beard, he altered his question: "You speak English?"
> Yes, the man said, he spoke English. He stood stiffly in the shade, a small man dressed in a shabby dark city suit, carrying a

small attache case. He had a novel under his arm: bits of an amorous scene stuck out, crudely coloured. He said: "Excuse me. I thought just now you were talking to me." He had protuberant eyes; he gave an impression of unstable hilarity, as if perhaps he had been celebrating a birthday . . . alone.

—GRAHAM GREENE, *The Power and the Glory*

"My good woman, we can't see you here without being alarmed for your safety. A stronger squall—"

She turned to look at him—or as it seemed to Charles, through him. It was not so much what was positively in that face which remained with him after that first meeting, but all that was not as he had expected; for theirs was an age when the favored feminine look was the demure, the obedient, the shy. Charles felt immediately as if he had trespassed....

—JOHN FOWLES, *The French Lieutenant's Woman*

Halfway down the subway stairs, he turned. He said, "'All things are lawful for me, but all things edify not.' One Corinthians ten."

As he spoke, his right eyelid fluttered part way down, then up again, and I thought he was winking. He was not. It was involuntary, just a lazy eyelid that slid partly shut sometimes.

He said, "We'll be seeing you," and then continued on down the stairs . . . .

Leo Bebb. He was all by himself, and because I had only that day for the first time met him face to face, I had no way of knowing who his *we* included.

—FREDERICK BUECHNER, *Lion Country*

A strong, distinctive, authoritative writing voice is something most fiction writers want—and something no editor or teacher can impart. It is, however, something any writer can bring out in himself or herself. But oddly enough, you can't bring out your writer's voice by concentrating on it.

A famous poet giving a series of seminars was once asked to read a poem by one of his students. The poem was a long, self-conscious allegory in which various guests at a party represented different aspects of the student's life. The poet read it, then handed it back with the comment, "No, kid. First write rhymy-dimey stuff."

We recently worked with a novelist whose fiction featured a lot of short, punchy sentences and partial sentences ("It's a quarter after one. Almost time. He runs a fingernail over a rough gouge coursing across the face of his watch, implanted by something in his fall. It still runs."). The result was a distinctive, high-tension voice, one the author had evidently put in a great deal of work to develop and maintain.

Unfortunately, the voice was so distinctive that all of his characters sounded alike. And the tension stayed at such a high pitch for so long that the novel became exhausting to read. It was rather like hearing "The Flight of the Bumblebee" expanded to concert length.

It's perfectly understandable that an author could fall in love with the work of a brilliant literary figure (William Faulkner, say, or William Burroughs) and then try to emulate that literary voice. But when an amateur author tries deliberately for the sort of mature voice found in seasoned professionals, the result is likely to be literarily pretentious and largely unreadable. In fact, this sort of literary pretentiousness is another clear mark of an amateur.

And what usually gets imitated in literary homage is the author's style, where the attempt (at least unconsciously) was to capture the author's voice. Style and voice are not interchangeable. If you think about it, you can see that every writer has or can have literary style, but by no means does every writer have a literary voice. And again, the way to develop voice is not by working on your style. Nor will using James Joyce's or Virginia Woolf's stylistic approaches give you their voices.

Bear in mind that most of the great stylists have developed their style in the service of their stories. Faulkner does some daring and original things with point of view and even tense in *As I Lay Dying*, and the style serves the story of the Bundrens very well. But when he's telling a simpler, more straightforward story (as in *The Reivers*) he uses a simpler, more straight-

"Remorse sits in my stomach like a piece of stale bread. How does that sound?"

forward style. Remember, your primary purpose as a writer of fiction is to engage your readers in your story, the best way you can. When your style starts to overshadow your story, it's defeating that purpose. No, kid, first write rhymy-dimey stuff.

The connection between a character's voice and an author's voice suggests another reason why conscious work on your writer's voice is often self-defeating. When you spend your creative energy in the service of the way your sentences read as prose, it's likely to be at the expense of your characters or story. Concentrate on your characters, concentrate on your story, and let your voice take care of itself.

After all, even those authors with the most distinctive voices did not develop those voices overnight. Melville simply couldn't have written *Omoo* in the voice he used in *Moby Dick*. He just wasn't ready yet. In order to write with a mature voice, you have to mature first.

But though you shouldn't consciously work on your voice as you write, there is a way to encourage it when you get to the self-editing stage. Start by rereading a short story, scene, or chapter as if you were reading it for the first time (rather as you would for the proportion exercise). Whenever you come to a sentence or phrase that gives you a little jab of pleasure, that makes you say "Ah, yes," that *sings*—highlight that passage in a color you like (we use yellow), or underline it. Then go through and read aloud all the sentences you highlighted or underlined. Don't analyze them for the moment, just try to absorb their rhythm or fullness or simplicity or freshness or whatever made them sing to you. What you've been reading aloud will represent, for now, your voice at its most effective. And making yourself conscious of it in this mechanical way will strengthen it.

Now read through the same section again, and when you come to those passages that make you wince—or just leave you cold—highlight the passage in a color you dislike, or draw a wavy line under the uninspired sentences. Go back and read consecutively all the passages you didn't like, and this time try to analyze what makes them different from the passages that sang to you. Is the writing flat? Strained? Awkward? Obvious? Pedestrian? Forced? Vague or abstract?

If flatness seems to be the problem, take a look at the surrounding sentences and see if they don't all have the same structure. Too many straight declarative sentences in a row, for instance, will flatten out anyone's writing. If the problem is abstraction or vagueness, rewrite for specificity. "A man walked into the room and ordered a drink" hasn't a fifth the bite of "A dwarf stepped up to the bar and ordered a bloody mary."

If the passage seems obvious, check for explanations—whether in dialogue, interior monologue, even narration—and

cut or rewrite accordingly. And if the writing seems strained or
forced or awkward, try reading the passage aloud—listening
carefully for any little changes you're inclined to make while
reading. More often than not, those changes will be in the
direction of your natural voice.

If you do this exercise often enough, you will develop a sen-
sitivity to your own voice that will gently encourage the development of the confidence and distinction you want. And this is
as true of character voice as it is of narrative voice. If you don't
pay meticulous detailed attention to the people you're writing
about, their voices can seem interchangeable. In the passages
that follow, taken from *The Company of Women*, Mary Gordon
gives us first-person narration from each major character in the
novel up to that point:

> It was because of the bats that I decided to marry.
> The attic of our house was infested with bats. And yet we care-
> fully avoided mentioning anything, out of some fairy-tale logic,
> for we knew that the first to speak would have to be the first to
> act. Cyprian was in the hospital. We were afraid he was dying.
> We were alone; we were women. We decided to be silent. Except
> my daughter, Linda. Daily, not less than three times a day for a
> week, she would say, "Something stinks in here." It was not I
> who taught her that diction. [Felicitas]

> I have never been happier in my life. Perhaps I should have
> been born an old woman; my talents have never been youthful
> ones . . . .
> The loss of Cyprian will be terrible, but I know about loss, and
> I no longer fear it. What I fear is that the center will not hold,
> that without him we will lose ourselves, that Felicitas and Leo
> will move off the land, and Clare will decide that life here is too
> dull for her, and Charlotte will stay with me reluctantly, out of
> duty. This is the proof of my selfish nature: I see the death of a
> man I have loved for forty years, who has guided my soul, who
> has kept me from terror and held back despair—I see his death

in terms of the breakup of the neighborhood. It is a child's fear, a child's egotism, and as the thought comes to me I pray the most childish of prayers: Let things stay as they are. [Charlotte]

Apart from him, I belong to no one; no one is fond of me except perhaps the child, and she would forget me in an hour. I must be seen, after he dies, as a burden, an unpaid debt.

So I am condemned to stay with them, homeless in my own home, suffered, borne, worse than a poor relation, for I am tied by no blood. There is nothing to bind me to them, only Cyprian, who has decided to die, leaving us to one another. [Muriel]

So I will bring my old age here [though] I may be bruised and grazed and wounded by the boredom, by the irritation and the crowding of domestic life. I fear the clips and stings of other human lives, lives less careful than my own. I fear the sound of Muriel's voice, the print of her green curtains; I fear Elizabeth's clumsiness and her uncertainties, Felicitas' rudeness and judgments, the ill-timed demands of Linda, the physical weakness of Cyprian . . . . I fear they will think my house is their house, that they can come in any time, sit anywhere, use anything. I am taking a risk, but in old age risk may be the only wise investment. [Clare]

I have had to learn the discipline of prosperous love, I have had to be struck down by age and sickness to feel the great richness of the ardent, the extraordinary love I live among. I have had to learn ordinary happiness, and from ordinary happiness, the first real peace of my life, my life which I had wanted full of splendor. I wanted to live in unapproachable light, the light of the pure spirit. Now every morning is miraculous to me. I wake and see in the thin, early light the faces of my friends.

And when I think of [those faces], I am tempted to work to prolong my life. [Cyprian]

Everyone is old here but my mother and me. All the people my mother loves are old but me. Soon they will die. That's why my mother wants to marry Leo. So that all the people she loves will not be old and dying . . . .

Now I see my mother leaning on her shovel; now I see my grandmother. They are laughing and they see me at the window. "Come out," they say, "come out and talk to us. We're lonely for you. Tell us something."

I run out. I can feel my heart. I am running toward them. They are standing under the apple tree. My mother picks me up and holds me in her arms. My grandmother is laughing. My mother lifts me up into the leaves. We are not dying. [Linda]

Every voice is distinct, because each one belongs to a character with a distinct personality and sensibility—this despite the fact that all of the characters are Catholic and most of them are elderly women with the same educational background. Every voice seems to arise spontaneously from the character rather than the author; nothing about the voices seems forced or unnatural.

Why? We doubt very much that it's because Mary Gordon sat down beforehand and worked out six different styles of speech and thought for six different characters. What's far more likely is that she has listened to her characters, has come to know them so intimately that one of them *can't* speak in the same voice as another.

"The limitation of the great stylists—Henry James, say, or Hemingway—" writes Frederick Buechner in *Spiritual Quests*, "is that you remember their voices long after you've forgotten the voices of any of the people they wrote about. In one of the Psalms, God says, 'Be still and know that I am God.' I've always taken that to be good literary advice, too. Be still the way Tolstoy is still, be still the way Anthony Trollope is still, so that your characters can become gods and speak for themselves and come alive in their own way."

In Chapter 4 we suggested reading aloud, consecutively, the

dialogue of each major character to encourage your distinguishing their voices. Well, reading aloud consecutively all the passages written from each major character's point of view can help you spot any places where the character's voice doesn't fit the character. Listen to what each one in turn says or thinks, and let your ear come up with the correction for anything that rings false to that character, any line of dialogue or thought that doesn't sound like what that character would say or think. Very often the character's voice will develop as much or more in the revision process than in the first draft.

And that's true for voice overall, as well. The greatest advantage of self-editing—including the highlighting procedure we've recommended in this chapter—is the kind of attention you have to pay to your own work while you're doing the self-editing. It demands that you revise again and again until what you've written rings true. Until you can believe it.

It invites you to listen to your own work. Do that job of listening carefully enough, lovingly enough, and you will start to hear your own writing voice.

CHECKLIST AND EXERCISES

Realistically, we can't really come up with a list of things to watch for as you improve your voice—there are no rules to becoming an individual. And the best exercise in developing your voice is to work on your own manuscript.

APPENDIX

....

ANSWERS TO EXERCISES

Actually, answers is a misnomer, since literature is not so much correct (or incorrect) as it is effective (or ineffective). You have almost certainly edited the exercises we've given you differently, and possibly more effectively, than we have. Still you might find it helpful to see what we've come up with.

CHAPTER 1

A. A fairly simple one to start with. The author breaks into the middle of a conversation to summarize one of the responses for us. Convert that bit of narrative summary into dialogue, and the scene works much better.

"Mortimer? Mortimer?" Simon Hedges said. "Where are you?"

"Look up, you ninny. I'm on the roof."

"What in blue blazes are you doing perched up there?"

"The cupola and weather vane finally got here," Mortimer said.

"I couldn't wait all day for you to install the gadgets, so here I am."

"How's it going so far?"

"I'm still sorting through the directions."

"Well, come on down before you kill yourself," Simon said. "I

swear I'll put them up for you this afternoon."

B. A slightly different approach to showing and telling. Rather than simply describing the effect the shop had on the narrator, describe the shop itself and let it have the same effect on the reader. As in:

I always figured I knew Uncle Zeb, until the day I walked into

his shop.

It was a small room, not much bigger than most kitchens. But

it was packed full of junk. No, not junk, junk isn't that well orga-

nized. *Stuff*. Two of the walls were covered floor to ceiling with

those metal shelves you see in library basements, and those

shelves were full of neat little boxes with labels like "Bearings

and Races" or "Angle Brackets, 3/8 and Larger."

And the tools! There was a drill press in one corner next to the

metal shelves and a lathe along the opposite wall. And a pegboard up above the workbench with two rows—two whole rows—of screwdrivers. There was a row of hammers—huge hammers with big flat heads and little bitty hammers with pointy heads, and some made out of rubber and some of lead. There were twenty-one different pairs of pliers (I counted), from big thick ones about a foot long to tiny things that were almost tweezers. There were tools I couldn't even recognize, things that had been made to do just one job and do it perfectly.

These weren't a handy person's tools. A handy person can keep all his tools in a drawer or in a box in the garage. Nope, Zeb was a craftsman.

C. *Of course, no two versions of this exercise are going to look exactly alike. Here's our take on the exercise:*

Roger realized he'd made a mistake about five minutes after he tried the short cut off of 9W. He'd been through about six intersections, and none of them had met at right angles.

He stopped to read a sign by the light of a streetlamp. Terpsichore Terrace. He didn't think he'd seen that one before, so he took a left.

Two lefts (Xanadu Drive, Lenape Lane), a right, (Camelot Court), and a few long, gentle curves later, he was back on Terpsichore Terrace. He couldn't be at the intersection he'd started at—he'd come too far for that. But the Blessed Virgin under the upturned bathtub in front of him did look familiar.

No, the other one had marigolds in front of it, and this one had . . . well . . . something else.

He pounded the steering wheel. All he wanted was a *street*. Something called "road" or "route," or even "avenue." Something with yellow lines down the middle. Something that went somewhere.

He parked, walked up to the Blessed Virgin's house and knocked. At least he could hope for a Christian reception.

"Yes?" The owner was elderly, balding, and wearing a cardigan in August.

"Sorry to bother you this late, but I seem to be a little twisted around. Can you tell me how to find 9W?"

"Of course. Let me see." The man stepped onto the porch and peered into the night. "What you want to do is turn around, then follow this road, Terpsichore Terrace, until it becomes Belleville

Drive. Then you would take the . . . let me see . . ." He began to tick them off on his fingers. "The fourth right—I can't recall the name of the street right now. Then the first left and follow that road until it ends."

Roger pointed. "This way until Belleville, fourth right, first left, follow to the end."

"That's all there is to it."

"Thanks."

Twenty minutes later Roger was facing a small, square house with a cast-iron deer in the front yard. On Xanadu Drive. Doubtless just a stone's throw from Terpsichore Terrace. He strode to the front door and pounded.

"Yeah?" Not elderly, still balding, tee shirt, no cardigan.

"Can I use your phone?"

"Yeah, sure."

Ten minutes later the taxi pulled up behind his car.

"What happened, Mac, you break down?"

"No, but I think I'm on the verge. I just want you to lead me back to 9W."

"No problem. 9W's about six bucks from here."

Roger paid the money gladly. "You don't seem surprised."

"Nah, why should I be? You're the third one so far this year."

CHAPTER 2

A. Exactly how you would convey Maggie's character through scenes depends, of course, on the plot of your story. You could show her lack of kinship with anybody but her own age group by giving her a linguistic quirk, some bit of slang or unusual phraseology that is shared by her friends and completely mystifying to everyone else.

And if your plot would allow it, there is real dramatic potential in revealing her character a little at a time. The beginning of the book could show only the more comic (and typical) aspects of her character—the restless energy, the boredom with everyone around her, the supercharged thoughts. Then, as the plot develops, you could start to show the fears behind the boredom, perhaps even including some hints of desperation. In short, you could turn Maggie into a real human being.

B. Again, the details of how to show the changes in the county depend on the details of your plot. One good approach would be to use the changes to the county as a backdrop for the story. For instance, you could have Fred get lost on his way to, say, his old high school because some of the roads he used then have become one-way. Or you could give him an occasional flashback to one of the family farms he remembers. Or you could simply have him express his disgust at the state of Route 59 to one of the other characters

CHAPTER 3

A. Okay, an easy one. The point of view essentially alternates between Ed and Susan. The first paragraph is clearly Susan's point of view since it contains her interior monologue. The third is from Ed's (same reason). "They had no time to lose" is practically omniscient narrator. When Susan is in the living room, she can't see Ed dashing around the kitchen. And after Ed ducks through the back door, he can't see Susan and the realtor's clients come in from the living room.

If you were to break the action up into different scenes separated by linespaces (as we did with the Harley example), each scene would only be a paragraph or so long. Since that's a bit short for a scene, a better approach might be to give everything from either Ed or Susan's point of view, or to have at most one break in mid-scene. You probably wouldn't want to use the omniscient narrator. You want your readers to feel the panic along with Ed and Susan, and the omniscient narrator would be too distancing.

So the answer is to pick one point of view or the other and stick with it. Perhaps Susan could hear Ed clanking around in the kitchen while she power-straightens the living room. Or perhaps Ed could hear Susan trying to lead the realtor upstairs as he ducks out the back door.

B. The point of view shifts here are more subtle. For one thing, Lance would be unlikely to think of a New York cab as a "New York cab," especially if he was a native New Yorker—he would just think of it as a "cab." We once had an author who used this technique to establish the locale of her story (in fact, she used the phrase, "New York cab"). But the damage done to the point of view usually isn't worth the information gained.

The second point of view problem arises because Lance, his nose in the newspaper, couldn't see the Park Avenue tunnel go by. And finally, when the cab pulls up to Grand Central (in itself enough to establish the New York location), Lance "disappears into the crowd." Since Lance never disappears as far as he is concerned, we lose his point of view.

In fact, these two paragraphs might almost be omniscient narration, except that there are hints of interior monologue ("That was fine with Lance . . ."). But even if the paragraphs were consistently omniscient, third person from Lance's point of view would still be more effective.

C. Let's try the first person first, writing from inside the head of an eight-year-old.

Miss Tessmacher was up at the board talking about subtraction or something. She'd just given us her pay-attention-you'll-need-this-when-you-grow-up lecture, so she wouldn't look this way for a while yet. Across the aisle, Sandy Dwerkin was working on a note to pass to Edith-the-hog Hoagland. I was leafing through my English reader looking for some pictures I maybe hadn't seen yet, when I happened to look out the window.

Snow!

All of a sudden, it was hard to sit still.

It was just a few little tiny flakes spitting down from the clouds and they wouldn't close the schools for it and it probably wouldn't even stick. But, jeez, it was only October and we were getting snow already. And maybe it *would* stick, it had been pretty cold lately, and the clouds looked serious—black and thick like they were going to be there a while.

Just until dismissal. Just through the rest of math and then English and then story time, that's all. If it would just keep snowing until then everything would be perfect.

Gosh, snow already!

Now let's try it from the omniscient. Since we're no longer limited to Mitch's perspective on life, we can make the narrative voice a bit more mature, even world-weary.

Of all the long and arbitrary divisions of the school day, fifth period is probably the hardest. Recess and lunch, along with the little bit of anticipation and excitement they can generate, are long since over. Dismissal is still two periods away, much too far ahead to even imagine. All that lies before the student, all that lay before Mitch, was the uninterrupted hard work of learning.

So, of course, it was a perfect time for the snow to begin.

The snowfall was hardly substantial, little more than a reminder that winter had arrived and a promise of what was to come. But that was far and away enough to fire Mitch's imagination with pictures of the coming season of sledding, snowball fights, and best of all school closings. Though he was not aware of them, there were even hints of the coming Christmas in his anticipation. Those few flakes represented the sea-change of the seasons, with all that it entailed.

Dismissal suddenly became delicious, and the long wait for the final bell all but unendurable.

And once more, from the third person.

Fifth period was always the hardest. Miss Tessmacher, up by the board, droned on about subtraction, Sandy Dwerkin scribbled a note to pass to Edith Hoagland, and Mitch flipped idly through his English book. A subtle motion outside caught the corner of his eye and he looked out the window next to his desk.

Snow!

The snow didn't amount to much—only an occasional spattering of delicate white flakes—but that didn't matter. Even though it was only October, autumn had turned a corner and become winter, with all that winter meant. Sledding, snowball fights with his sister, even school closings, were all right there in those few little flakes. If only it would last until dismissal.

Suddenly he found it hard to sit still.

D. Let's try it first from Maggie's point of view.

Maggie glanced at her watch again. Brad had said he'd, like, call at six, and here it was four and they weren't finished yet. God, Christmas shopping was a drag.

And now her mom was looking down the aisle toward the toy

section. "Why don't we pick up something nice for your brother while we're here?"

"Ma, we got the rest of the week to shop for Mitch. Come on, okay?"

"Don't rush me. This will only take a minute, and it might save us a trip later."

Yeah, right, like the half-hour in the shoe store was only going to take a minute.

But there was nothing else to do, so Maggie tagged behind her mother through aisle after aisle of plastic junk. Baby junk, toddler junk, Fisher-Price junk (two aisles of that), Lego junk. Finally they came to the aisle little Mitchy-mitch always dragged them to when they went shopping—action-figure junk.

Her mom was staring around her at plastic figures in primary colors with, like, *huge* biceps. God, like any of the men she knew actually looked like that.

"What do you think Mitch would like, dear?"

She grabbed one of the figures at random. "What about this one? He'll love it."

Her mom peered at the package. "Oh, I don't know, doesn't he already have all of those turtle things?"

"No, Ma, this one's new. All the kids are getting it."

"I don't know—"

"Come on, Ma. I'm, like, almost absolutely positively certain this is the one that will finish off his collection. Can we get it, please?"

"All right, then."

"Great. I'll go get on line at the register." And she was gone down the aisle while she had a chance.

And from Mom's POV.

Eloise paused in front of the registers. So far they'd bought for Roger and Edna and all of their brood. And Maggie's present was safely stowed away in the basement (that child was *so* hard to shop for). And Reginald was at home now trying to assemble that action-figure play set thing for Mitch—was it a Star Wars ship or Star Trek or was it something to do with the turtles?

And what else was there to buy? What was she forgetting? Oh, yes, stocking stuffers.

"Why don't we pick up something nice for your brother while we're here?"

"Ma, we got the rest of the week to shop for Mitch," Maggie said. "Come on, okay?"

"Don't rush me. This will only take a minute, and it might save us a trip later."

Honestly, Maggie had been antsy all day. How could a child who begged to go to the mall so often hate shopping so much?

Still, Maggie followed along through the huge and bewildering toy section. Aisle after aisle of toys arranged more or less in chronological order, from rattles and teething rings to electric trains and computers. Imagine, a computer as a toy. Finally they came to the action-figures. There seemed to be armies of them in their packages.

"What do you think Mitch would like, dear?"

"What about this one?" Maggie handed her a small green man with a colored mask. "He'll love it."

"Oh, I don't know. Doesn't he already have all of those turtle things?" Heaven knows they all looked alike.

"No, Ma, this one's new. All the kids are getting it."

"I don't know—"

"Come on, Ma. I'm almost absolutely positively certain this is the one that will finish off his collection. Can we get it, please?"

"All right, then."

"Great. I'll go get on line at the register."

And before Eloise could say a word, Maggie was tearing off through the aisles. There was nothing she could do but try to keep up.

CHAPTER 4

A. A fairly easy one to begin with. Lots of unusual speaker attributions, some repetition, a few -lys. A little too much direct address, more speaker attributions than are strictly needed. And note that the chuckling has been converted from a speaker attribution to a beat. Most of the editing is simply cutting, and the results look like this.

"You aren't seriously thinking about putting that trash in your body, are you?"

I put down the package of Twinkies and turned around. It was Fred McDermot, a passing acquaintance from work.

"Pardon me?" I said.

"You heard me."

I chuckled. "Fred, I can't for the life of me see why this is any of your business."

"I'm just thinking of you, that's all," he said. "Do you know what they put in those things?"

"No."

"Neither do I. That's the point."

B. *Of course, it's a risky business trying to rewrite a classic like* Gatsby. *And some of you will probably feel we have edited some of the character out of the book, some of the lushness that makes it the novel it is. Well, we do believe there's room for lushness in a novel, but not in the dialogue mechanics. And no matter how much of a genius Fitzgerald may have been, when he writes "he assured us positively," he is not at his best. After all, can you assure someone negatively?*

Here's our re-edit of an American classic:

"I like to come," Lucille said. "I never care what I do, so I always have a good time. When I was here last, I tore my gown on a chair, and he asked me my name and address—within a week I got a package from Croirier's with a new evening gown in it."

"Did you keep it?" asked Jordan.

"Sure I did. I was going to wear it tonight, but it was too big in the bust and had to be altered. It was gas blue with lavender beads. Two hundred and sixty-five dollars."

"There's something funny about a fellow that'll do a thing like that," said the other girl. "He doesn't want any trouble with *any*body."

"Who doesn't?" I asked.

"Gatsby. Somebody told me..."

The two girls and Jordan leaned their heads together.

"Somebody told me they thought he killed a man."

A thrill passed over all of us. The three Mr. Mumbles bent forward in their seats.

"I don't think it's so much *that*," Lucille said. "It's more that he was a German spy during the war."

One of the men nodded.

"I heard that from a man who knew all about him, grew up with him in Germany," he said.

"Oh, no," said the first girl, "it couldn't be that, because he was in the American army during the war. You look at him sometimes when he thinks nobody's looking at him. I'll bet he killed a man."

CHAPTER 5

A. Four sailors shooting the breeze in complete, precise, well-rounded sentences. There were two little speeches, the first paragraph and the next to last, which we broke up with some give and take and by distributing the dialogue among the characters. We got rid of the scare quotes (which we'll get into in Chapter 11), and also threw in a few contractions and one profanity for good measure. As edited, the scene runs:

As they sat quietly catching their breath, Getz turned to Wheeler. "Kid, we've all been diving together a long time and are real comfortable with each other. You're new. We hear you're good, but you're still new."

"What's your point?"

"You wouldn't object to a question or two, would you?"

"Ask away."

"What's your maximum no-decompress bottom time at three atmospheres?"

"The U.S. Navy tables allow sixty minutes at sixty feet with a standard rate of ascent. How's that?"

"Good enough, " Nick said. "Welcome aboard."

"No offense, kid," Getz said. "We're generally more than ten hours from a doctor and there's no recompression chamber in the whole damn country. We can't afford to push the tables."

Lou grinned. "You mean we can't afford to *regularly* push the tables."

B. This one is rather like one of those "what's wrong with this picture" puzzles. You can see there are a lot of problems. The challenge lies in catching all of them. As edited, the scene reads like this:

I peered through the front window of the garage, which did me no good because light hadn't been able to penetrate that window since man landed on the moon.

I tapped on the door. "Anybody here?"

A man came out from the shop wearing greasy, half-unzipped coveralls with the name "Lester" stitched in over the pocket. I hoped he took those off before he got into my car. Lester took his cigar stub out of his mouth and spat near my feet.

"Yeah, what can I do you for?"

"Well, my name is Mr. Baumgarten. I'm here to pick up my car. Is it ready?"

"Hang on a sec." He stepped back into the shop and picked up a greasy clipboard with a thick wad of forms under the clip. "What was the name again, Bumgarden?"

"BAUMgarten." You cretin.

"Yeah, right." He pawed through the forms. "Don't see you here, Mr. BAUMgarden. Sorry."

"What do you mean, sorry? You have my car in there. Either it's fixed or it's not."

"Look, mister, what do you think, I got time to get, like, intimate with all my clientele? You could be Baumgarden, you could be his cousin, you could be Governor Cuomo for all I know."

"I'd be happy to show you my driver's—"

"It don't matter. I ain't giving you no car unless you got papers and I got matching papers. Far as I'm concerned, you ain't on this clipboard, you don't exist."

CHAPTER 6

A. Yes, that's right, we've thrown in a few points from previous chapters, just to keep you on your toes (and did you catch the point of view shift?). As to the interior monologue itself, there is way too much of it—after all, did Kimberly just stand there while she went over Ed's organizational habits in her head? There are also too many speaker attributions (he thought) and otherwise awkward mechanics. So, as edited, the passage looks like this:

"Excuse me, miss, but I'm giving a seminar over in Room 206 in a few minutes and I need an overhead projector."

The guy at the door of the audio-visual room was actually wearing a tweed jacket with leather patches at the elbows. My God, typical English professor. All he needs is a pipe.

"Okay, if you want an overhead or something like that—a movie projector or slides or whatever—you have to fill out a form ahead of time," Kimberly said. "Then we can, like, line everything up and—"

"I know. I sent in the form three weeks ago."

"You've been up to the seminar room?" she said.

"Yes, and the projector wasn't there."

Okay, great. She only took over from Ed yesterday and here was her first major screw-up. "Okay, do you have your, what do you call it, your course form?"

He snapped the briefcase open and pulled out the familiar green card. "Right here."

"Yeah, give me a minute."

She ducked into the office and dug out the clipboard with all the requisitions on it. A few minutes later, the guy stuck his head in the office.

"Miss, will this take much longer? I don't want to be late."

"What's the course number."

"A3205."

She went through the forms again. Definitely no A3205 there.

"What's the room number."

"As I believe I told you, it's 206. I don't suppose you could just give me a projector now, could you? I'd be happy to carry it over myself."

"Nope, we don't have any to spare. If you want one, we have to figure out where yours went."

One more time through the forms, and there it was. "Okay, here's the problem. I have Room 206 listed as A9631, 'Making Fresh Baby Food at Home.' The projector should be up there."

"Miss, the projector's not there. That's why I'm here."

Jeez, what did it take to please this guy? "You're sure it's not there? Did you check the closet?"

"Room 206 doesn't have a closet."

"Sure it does. The big seminar room off the cafeteria, right?"

"No, it's a smallish room near the elevators. How long have you worked here?"

"Long enough to know the building. Did you come across the courtyard to get here?"

"Um, yes, I did."

"Okay, look, we don't handle that wing of the building from here. You want the AV room for the Peebles annex, it's down by the bursar's office."

"Oh, I see." He looked at his watch. "Well, thank you."

"Hey, no sweat. We're here to serve."

B. Of course, there are too many italics. But the real point of this exercise is that very little of the actual interior monologue was cut. After all, the point of the scene is the contrast between what Norm is thinking and what he says, and you just can't do that as dialogue. So we just recast the interior monologue in the third person and here's the result:

Norm looked at the finished door frame for the patio doors. All he had to do now was hang the doors themselves, then after the electrician futzed around for a few more days the living room would be ready for drywall. It was his favorite stage in a construction project— when the place he was building began to actually look like a house.

"Excuse me, Norm?"

"Yes, Mrs. Kincaid." The homeowner. There was nothing he loved more than to have the homeowner on site at this stage in the game.

"I was wondering, will the doors actually be that narrow?"

And this was why. "Yes ma'am, I'm afraid so."

"Do you suppose we could make them a little bit wider? Not

much, say a foot or so on each side?"

Ah, the joy of cost overruns. He'd just remove those two load-

bearing members—he could probably get away with it if he rein-

forced the corner posts and ran an I-beam between them. It

would mean restructuring the entire front of the house, but he

could do it. And then he'd throw away those custom-made doors

and have some new ones custom made.

"Well, it might cost a little extra."

"Oh, but I think it would be worth it. Just imagine the extra

light the wider doors would bring."

Yeah. Just imagine the yacht he'd buy with the proceeds.

"All right, ma'am, I'll get right on it."

*C. Again, we're editing some brilliant authors, which is a little
risky. But then, the better the writers, the more they deserve careful
editing. So here's our take on these five authors:*

There ought to be a whole separate language for words that are

truer than other words—for perfect, absolute truth. It was the purest

fact of her life: she did not understand him, and she never would.

—ANNE TYLER, *Dinner at the Homesick Restaurant*

"You see," Smiley said, "our obsession with virtue won't go away. Self-interest is so *limiting*. So is expediency." He paused again, still deep inside his own thoughts. "All I'm really saying, I suppose, is that if the temptation to humanity does assail you now and then, I hope you won't take it as a weakness in yourselves but give it a fair hearing." Of course, the cufflinks. George was remembering the old man.

—JOHN LE CARRÉ, *The Secret Pilgrim*

"Did you go up there? When you were young?"

"I went to dances," the doctor said. "I specialized in getting Cokes for people. I was extremely good at getting Cokes passed around." He helped her into a chair. "Now, then, what can I do for you?"

Amanda sat her pocketbook down on the floor and told him what she had come for.

Jesus Christ. How many years did he have to practice medicine before he learned never to be surprised at anything?

—ELLEN GILCHRIST, *The Annunciation*

This wasn't Dalgleish's case and he couldn't stop him by force. But at least he could ensure that the direct path to the body lay undisturbed. Without another word he led the way and Mair followed.

Why this insistence on seeing the body? To satisfy himself that she was in fact, dead, the scientist's need to verify and confirm? Or was he trying to exorcise a horror he knew could be more terrible in imagination than in reality? Or was there, perhaps, a deeper compulsion, the need to pay her the tribute of standing over her body in the quietness and loneliness of the night before the police arrived with all the official paraphernalia of a murder investigation to violate forever the intimacies they had shared?

—P D. JAMES, *A Taste for Death*

Of course Owen had the ball. He was a collector; one had to consider only his baseball cards.

"After all," Mr. Chickering would say—in later years—"it was the only decent hit the kid ever made, the only real wood he ever got on the ball. And even then, it was a foul ball. Not to mention that it killed someone."

But so what if Owen had the ball?

—JOHN IRVING, *A Prayer for Owen Meany*

CHAPTER 7
A. *At least one beat between every line of dialogue, some of them clichés (kicking the tire, for instance) and some of them simply too*

*detailed (three separate actions to open the hood). Try the scene
again with the deadwood gone.*

"You're sure it runs?" Mr. Dietz said.

I leaned against the fender. "It did last time I tried it."

"Yeah, well, when was that."

"Just last week. Here, listen."

I hopped in the front seat and hit the starter. The engine
caught, then sputtered and died. I pumped the gas once or twice
and tried again. This time it caught and purred.

"Well, I don't know. It sounds all right, but I don't like the
looks of the body." He kicked the fender. Little flakes of rust
dropped to the ground.

"Look, for three hundred dollars, what do you want?" I revved it
a little. "I mean, listen to that, it's running like a baby. You should
get twenty thousand miles out of this with no trouble. At least
twenty."

He peered into one of the wheel wells. "As long as one of the
tires doesn't fall off on me."

"There's a spare in the trunk. So what do you say?"

B. Now for one where you have to put the beats in. In this particular example, the beats help add a sense of rhythm to the dialogue, to show some of the hesitance that can come with strong emotion.

"Do you really think this is a smart move?" she said. "I mean, you don't know anybody in California."

"I'm pretty sure." She could see him lying there in the moonlight, hands behind his head, staring at the ceiling. "After all, it's not as if I have a choice. You've got to go where the jobs are."

"What about the kids?"

He rolled to face her. "Honey, it's not like I'm going to be gone forever. I'll send for you as soon as I can."

"Yeah, but when will that be? Where are you going to stay, what are you going to do, how are you going to live there?"

"I'm taking the tent, and I can sleep in the car if need be. Besides, I'll find something within a week, you can count on it."

"I . . . " Her hands were knotted in the sheet. She forced herself to let go. "It's just that I'm scared."

He reached out to her and brushed back a wisp of hair that had fallen over one eye. "I know. So am I."

CHAPTER 8

A. Of course, there are no real answers to this exercise.

B. New paragraphs for new speakers, trim back on the beats a little, and break up the longer speeches with some give-and-take or by running two sentences together into one.

Jeannine stared at the spider plant hung over the kitchen sink. Most of its leaves were yellow and a few were going brown at the edges.

"I don't believe this," she said.

"What?" Ed said.

"I only gave you this plant a month ago, and look at it." She reached out and tenderly touched one of the leaves. It came off in her hand. "I mean, spider plants thrive on neglect. How did you manage to do this much damage so quickly?"

"I don't know. I've been watering it once a week, just like you said. I've even been using plant food I picked up at the hardware store the other day."

"What kind of plant food?"

"It's that blue powder that dissolves in water, one tablespoon to the quart."

One tablespoon? "Ed, let me see that plant food."

He opened the cupboard under the sink, rummaged around for a moment, and came up with a box with a picture of a rose on front. She took it and scanned the instructions.

"According to this, you're supposed to use one teaspoon to the quart."

"Oh, well, I guess that explains it, then."

CHAPTER 9

A. A funny idea undone by overkill. With a little less detail on the social graces of a bachelor's apartment, the scene works much better. Also, notice that we changed the velvet couch to satin, just to get rid of the repetition of "velvet."

"Come on in, don't be bashful."

It wasn't exactly bashfulness that was keeping me in the hallway. This was my first visit to a bachelor's apartment, and I was shocked at how much it lived up to the reputation.

It wasn't just the velvet painting of Elvis on the wall above the blue satin couch, or the orange shag rug, or even the brown recliner with the cigarette burns in front of the TV. It was the unidentified stains on the ceiling that made me wonder. Those and the nicks in the top of the formica coffee table that looked as if they might have been caused by tap shoes. Also the TV antenna was a bent coathanger with an undershirt hanging from it, presumably a dirty undershirt though I didn't want to get close enough to check.

"Like it?" he said. "I spent all day yesterday cleaning it up, just for you."

B. Again, we need to hear something of Clancy, but the author tells us how boring he is once or twice too often—especially considering that he's a minor character we don't meet again. As edited, the passage reads:

Clancy is a referral from Marilyn Reinhold via Donald Grayson via Rose Sumner. It doesn't speak well for my colleagues, passing the man around that way, not that I blame them. There are so many interesting people in this city who get into therapy—trisexual television producers, addicted actresses, ad agency workaholics, manic-depressive Wall Street dynamos—it hardly seems necessary to suffer through a patient like Clancy. An accountant for a small rock salt distributor in Queens, he's a timid man with a nasal, rambling speaking style, so slow you could doze off before he gets the next word out. Usually the words are about his employer of ten years, who pays him $22,000 per year, expects

overtime without pay, and for some reason has Clancy's undying

allegiance. Clancy's really a nice man, but his problems are

small, very small.

CHAPTER 10
A. The author here simply spends too much time on characters the readers are never going to meet again. All we really need is a glimpse of them in passing, as in:

As he approached the last hill, Carter passed another runner

who had started fast but was now spent and fading, his once crisp

stride now a weary shuffle.

CHAPTER 11
A. Somehow our compunctions about editing a master weren't as strong on this exercise as in the past. Here are the results:

She grabbed up a pelt, pulled it close about her, and gave him

an impishly wicked grin. Then she turned on her heels with a low

laugh, went to the hearth, and lay three small logs on the still

warm coals. She blew upon them but drew back in haste when

the ashes flew up.

Wulfgar's amused chuckles filled the room. She made a face at

him and swung the kettle of water on its hook over the building heat. He crossed to the warmth of the fire beside her and began to dress.

B. The trick, of course, is to get rid of the unusual speaker attributions and interior monologue mechanics and still preserve the flavor of the original. For what it's worth, here's our version:

All this time Tweedledee was trying his best to fold up the umbrella with himself in it, which was such an extraordinary thing to do that it quite took Alice's attention off the angry brother. Tweedledee's attempts ended in his rolling over, bundled up in the umbrella, with only his head out. And there he lay, opening and shutting his mouth and his large eyes, looking more like a fish than anything else.

"Of course you agree to have a battle?" Tweedledum said in a calmer tone.

"I suppose so." The other crawled out of the umbrella. "Only *she* must help us dress up, you know."

So the two brothers went off hand in hand into the wood and returned in a minute with their arms full of things—bolsters, blankets, hearthrugs, tablecloths, dish covers, and coal scuttles.

"I hope you're a good hand at pinning and tying strings?" Tweedledum said. "Every one of these things has got to go on, somehow or other."

Alice had never seen such a fuss made about anything in all her life—the way those two bustled about, and the quantity of things they put on, and the trouble they gave her in tying strings and fastening buttons. *Really, they'll be more like bundles of old clothes than anything else by the time they're ready*.

"Arrange that bolster round my neck," Tweedledee said.

"What will this do?" Alice draped the bolster around him as best she could.

"Do? Why, it will keep my head from being cut off, of course. You know, it's one of the most serious things that can possibly happen to one in a battle, to get one's head cut off."

C. Yes, they're all in there. With the description of the pizza man, we even managed to work a proportion problem into a single-page exercise.

"But Ernestine, honey, I swear I was never anywhere near the John Smith motel."

"Not according to Helena," Ernestine said.

Winthrop felt like a small boy with a baseball bat in front of a broken window. A boy who hadn't broken the window.

"Ernestine, you've got better sense than to listen to a trouble-making fool like Helena Basquette. Why, only last week—"

The doorbell rang.

Ernestine propped her cigar on the ashtray at her arm and went to the door.

A tall young man held out a steaming, fragrant box.

"You the guys ordered the pizza?"

"Winthrop, *sweetie*," Ernestine called over her shoulder, "are you responsible for this?"

READING LIST

....

BOOKS

Applebaum, Judith, *How to Get Happily Published: A Complete and Candid Guide* (HarperCollins, 1991). There are half a dozen books in print on this subject; this one lives up to its subtitle. Immensely helpful to nonfiction as well as fiction writers.

Block, Lawrence, *Writing the Novel: From Plot to Print* (Writer's Digest Books, 1979). An engaging step-by-step guide by the creator of the Matthew Scudder mystery series. Particularly helpful on the psychological processes and the pitfalls involved in writing a novel.

————, *Telling Lies for Fun and Profit* (Writer's Digest Books, 1981). A nuts-and-bolts book on fiction technique, one of the very best.

————, *Spider, Spin Me a Web: Lawrence Block on Writing Fiction* (Writer's Digest Books, 1988). The best book available on balancing, intertwining, combining, and interweaving fiction elements to engage—enweb—the reader. We found it also inspirational and supportive of the writer (whether fiction or nonfiction).

Bocca, Geoffrey, *You Can Write a Novel* (Spectrum, 1983). A lively and often helpful book combining fiction technique theory and nuts-and-bolts advice/encouragement for the beginning writer.

Brown, Rita Mae, *Starting from Scratch* (Bantam, 1988). Quirky, insightful views on fiction writing by a best-selling novelist.

Card, Orson Scott, *Characters and Viewpoint* (Writer's Digest Books, 1981). A thoroughgoing consideration of the advantages and disadvantages of different point-of-view choices.

Conrad, Barnaby, *The Complete Guide to Writing Fiction* (Writer's Digest Books, 1990). Wonderfully helpful theory and technique discussions by the director of the Santa Barbara Writer's Conference and a wide range of well-known, articulate fiction craftsmen—from Alice Adams to Elmore Leonard to Eudora Welty.

Gardner, John, *The Art of Fiction: Notes on Craft for Young Writers* (Random House, 1991). Fiction technique theory by the late novelist and writing instructor. Despite the subtitle, veteran fiction writers will find it worth reading.

————, *On Becoming a Novelist* (Harper & Row, 1983). A provocative, authoritative manual on fiction craft by the late writing instructor.

Goldberg, Natalie, *Writing Down the Bones* (Shambhala, 1986). An inspirational book about the process of "uneducation" and its potential for releasing creativity in the fiction writer. No nuts-and-bolts technique here; this is the writer's equivalent of *Zen and the Art of Motorcycle Maintenance*.

Goldfarb, Ronald L. and Gail E. Ross, *The Writer's Lawyer* (Times Books, 1989). Candid, immensely helpful legal advice for writers, covering everything from the first amendment to the wording of the book contract.

Hall, Oakley, *The Art and Craft of Novel Writing* (Writer's Digest Books, 1989). Despite its title, craft rather than art is the focus here. As such, it is instructive as well as inspirational—this experienced writing teacher draws his examples from masters of their genres, from William Faulkner to John Irving to Arthur Hailey.

Hughes, Elaine Farris, *Writing from the Inner Self* (Harper-Collins, 1991). A series of meditative techniques designed to unblock writers and help them learn to write from the subconscious. Delivers what it promises.

Noble, William, *"SHUT UP!" He Explained: A Writer's Guide*

to the Uses and Misuses of Dialogue (Paul S. Eriksoon, 1987). Particularly helpful to fiction writers seeking to improve their dialogue content.

Swain, Dwight V., *Creating Characters: How to Build Story People* (Writer's Digest, 1990). Provocative, helpful advice on strengthening characters from the perspective of what the characters care about.

Zinsser, William, *On Writing Well* (4th edition, Harper-Collins, 1990). The indispensable guide to writing nonfiction, with useful applications to fiction on such subjects as writing with a word processor, usage, sexism, organization, and attitudes toward language and craft.

———, *Writing to Learn: How to Write—and Think—Clearly About Any Subject At All* (HarperCollins, 1991). Zinsser's deservedly classic guide can help any writer at all, whether beginner or veteran, writing fiction or nonfiction.

COMPUTER SOFTWARE

WritePro: An interactive computer program for creating believable characters, dramatic plot, effective dialogue, suspenseful scenes. The only creative-writing software selected by the Book-of-the-Month club and the Literary Guild.

First Aid for Writers: Described by *The New York Times* as "a combination program for both fiction and nonfiction writers to help in solving the kinds of problems that practicing writers commonly encounter in planning, writing, and revising their work."

For information on computer software, call (800) 755-1124.

INDEX

ABOUT THE AUTHORS

RENNI BROWNE has been a book editor for thirty years, during which she worked as an editor for Charles Scribner and Sons and senior editor for Stein and Day and William Morrow & Co. In 1978 she left mainstream publishing to resume editing books instead of making deals and courting literary agents. In 1980 she founded The Editorial Department, Inc., a company of independent book editors based in Los Angeles and New York. The company evaluates and edits the work of many well-established writers and first-time novelists, over half of whom eventually get published. She divides her time between Grandview-on-the-Hudson, New York, and the foothills of the Blue Ridge mountains in East Tennessee.

DAVE KING joined The Editorial Department in 1987, bringing with him a degree in philosophy and years of experience as a geological lab technician, science writer, and computer programmer. His fiction specialties are science fiction, mysteries, contemporary fiction, and historical fiction. He lives on a farm in upstate New York.

Renni and Dave are among those Editorial Department editors who give writers' workshops around the country on self-editing, fiction technique, publishing strategies, inspirational writing, dialogue, mystery and suspense technique, and other topics.